CREATING
DAIRYLAND

Welcome to Wisconsin!
All ye who wish to toil;
Vast harvests are awaiting
The tillers of her soil.
Welcome to Wisconsin!
All ye who come for gain;
An empire's wealth lies hidden
Within her wide domain.
Welcome to Wisconsin!
All ye who would be free;
The justice she dispenses
Is famed from sea to sea.
Welcome to Wisconsin!
All ye who seek the chance
To join the van of progress
In the world's new renaissance.

William Dawson, Madison, Wisconsin
March 30, 1914

How caring for cows

saved our soil,

created our landscape,

brought prosperity to our state,

and still shapes our way of life in Wisconsin

CREATING
DAIRYLAND

Edward Janus

Wisconsin Historical Society Press

Published by the Wisconsin Historical Society Press
Publishers since 1855

© 2011 by the State Historical Society of Wisconsin

For permission to reuse material from *Creating Dairyland*, 978-0-87020-463-0,
please access www.copyright.com or contact the Copyright Clearance Center, Inc. (CCC), 222
Rosewood Drive, Danvers, MA 01923, 978-750-8400. CCC is a not-for-profit organization that
provides licenses and registration for a variety of users.

wisconsin**history**.org

Photographs identified with WHi or WHS are from the Society's collections; address requests to
reproduce these photos to the Visual Materials Archivist at the Wisconsin Historical Society, 816
State Street, Madison, WI 53706.

Front cover image: *Dairy Farming* by Richard Jansen. Installed in the Reedsburg, Wisconsin,
post office in 1940. Photo by Mark Fay.

Frontmatter photo credits: frontispiece, photo by Jerry Quebe; page viii, WHi Image ID 76306

Printed in Wisconsin, U.S.A.

Design by Diana Boger

15 14 13 12 11   1 2 3 4 5

LIBRARY OF CONGRESS CATALOGING-IN-PUBLICATION DATA
Janus, Edward.
Creating Dairyland : how caring for cows saved our soil, created our
landscape, brought prosperity to our state, and still shapes our way of life
in Wisconsin / Edward Janus.
  p. cm.
Includes bibliographical references and index.
ISBN 978-0-87020-463-0 (pbk. : alk. paper) 1. Dairy farming—
Wisconsin—History. 2. Dairy farming—Social aspects—Wisconsin—
History. 3. Dairy farming—Environmental aspects—Wisconsin—History.
4. Dairy farmers—Wisconsin— Interviews. 5. Cheesemakers—Wisconsin—
Interviews. 6. Farm life—Wisconsin. 7. Wisconsin—Social life and customs.
8. Wisconsin—Environmental conditions. 9. Wisconsin—Biography.
10. Oral history—Wisconsin. I. Title.
SF232.W6J3 2011
636.2'14209775—dc22
                              2010039307

∞ The paper used in this publication meets the minimum requirements of the American
National Standard for Information Sciences—Permanence of Paper for Printed Library Materials,
ANSI Z39.48–1992.

Publication of this book was made possible in part by a grant from the John C. Geilfuss fellowship
fund.

To Ernest and Joseph Haugen, dairy farmers:
Thank you for showing me the true and ancient face
of Wisconsin dairying. This book is dedicated to you and
the thousands of others like you, whose steadfast,
quiet, and worthy work created Dairyland.

Contents

ↄ

6913, 'Tis the Land of Liberty, flowing with milk and Honey.

Acknowledgments

༈

Like any book of history and nonfiction, this one is mostly a report of the lives and ideas of others. Without the countless men and women who milked our cows, made our cheese, and created our landscape, I would have no story to tell. I first and foremost want you to know that this book was really "written" by those who lived the lives and thought the thoughts I only report here. Although most of their voices have been quieted, I hope this book will remind us that they prepared the soil from which we grow today. They, not this book, deserve praise.

Naturally I want to thank the people who so generously sat down and talked with me at length about their work and lives. Alas, there were just not enough pages to include all of you here, but what you told me has been as important to this story as those voices I've been able to include. My sessions with you gave me insights that I could never have gotten from books. Thank you all! My life is richer for my having talked with you.

I wish to acknowledge my debt to Eric Lampard, the author of what is no doubt the most important work on the dairy history of our state, *The Rise of the Dairy Industry in Wisconsin*. Thank you.

Like many journalists, I start a project with only a dangerously limited understanding of my subject. But I've been very lucky indeed to have extremely tolerant people to disabuse me of my ignorance. I'd especially like to thank my friend Laura Daniels, the epitome of Wisconsin progressive dairying. Laura still accepts my calls for help when I need to know about cows' stomachs or their feed or any number of questions. Thanks again, Laura. Likewise to Bob Cropp, ag agent in Pepin County, and my friend the dairy journalist John

Oncken, the man who knows more dairy history than anyone. These folks, I want you to know, are not responsible for the things I have gotten wrong in this book. They all tried to educate me. It just may not be possible.

I want to thank Patrick Geoghegan, vice president of the Wisconsin Milk Marketing Board, for believing that I had something important to say about dairying. Patrick and the WMMB understand as well as anyone that explaining our wonderful dairy industry to people outside of dairying is important, because otherwise they would be missing one of the great stories in Wisconsin history. For your belief in the wonderfulness of the dairy story and your faith in me that I could help tell it, thanks! And thanks too to Heather Porter Engwall at the WMMB for your help in getting to know today's dairy folks and for your enthusiasm for this story.

Now to the saint disguised as my editor Kate Thompson. I have decided to never open my mouth again without checking with you first. Everyone in life needs a good editor, and I got one. Thank you for keeping my sometimes quirky voice, and thank you especially for making this book better. I trust that is the highest thing an author can say of his editor.

And finally, to Mary: I bet you think you've heard the last of ancient silos and cows as avatars. Maybe! But thanks for listening all these years.

Introduction

❧

READING DAIRYLAND

Photo by Mark Fay

They serve God well who care for His creatures.
—A. J. Philips, *Queen Vashti: The Autobiography of a Guernsey Cow*

CARE OF THE cow has brought prosperity to Wisconsin.

And in a very important way, I believe the dairy cow *created* Wisconsin—that is, created the Wisconsin we know and love today. For when we drive through Dairyland we take in a scene that truly defines us: the neat barns with their ranks of silos, the undulating

A farmer's feet are well planted in the stuff of dairying.

green of grasses, and especially the cows, our avatars of contentment. All of this—our farms, their silos and cows; our farmers, their prosperity and their intelligence; all the fields of grass; and our remarkable history—make up what I like to call the book of Dairyland.

During the 160 years since dairy cows began to reshape Wisconsin's landscape, economics, moral ethic, and way of life, many thousands of men and women have been initiated into a kind of faith: faith that care of the cow and the soil would bring them prosperity, even happiness. These are people who lived with mud, manure, and milk on their boots. They and thousands of their children and grandchildren have wanted nothing more than to stay on their land with their cows. Why that is so, and how it has been possible, is the story I hope to tell. It is one of the great stories of Wisconsin.

I got mud, manure, and milk on my boots for the first time in 1973, when I became a novice dairyman on a thirty-cow farm in Crawford County. And although I no longer wear boots, that milk remains indelibly on my soul.

How else can I describe what happened to me on those warming June mornings when I went up the hill at 5:00 a.m. to find our cows grazing in their companionable groups, as cows had been doing long before humans came along? Or how I felt on the Christmas Eve when I delivered a calf in our midnight-stilled barn, alone except for the thirty mothers quietly watching and chewing? I can't argue with miracles.

During the too-brief time I spent on the farm, I enjoyed many cups of coffee and plates overloaded with pork chops in my neighbors' kitchens. I spent many hours loading hay with the bachelor neighbor down the road. I watched with admiration as the farmers in our co-op practiced democracy.

I was impressed by how intellectual the progressive farmers in our area were about the business of caring for cows; how avidly they read the latest research on feed and making cows comfortable; how they kept detailed records and charted their progress, learned from experts in nutrition and agronomy, and visited their most successful neighbors to learn their secrets. These progressive men and women taught me that dairy farming is as much about thinking as it is about mud, milk, and manure.

I also deeply appreciated our neighbors who were not exactly progressive, those who cared for their cows and their land as they had learned to do from their fathers. These were farmers for whom *the way things are* is just fine—men and women content, I thought, to stay within the closed universe of barn, pasture, and misty field, to find a degree of satisfaction by playing only their own small part in the world.

I saw how deeply committed our neighbors were to their land and to passing on a more fertile, improved farm to their children. And I was surprised, and impressed, by how often their children wanted to stay on the farm. But by then I was coming to understand that dairy farming is likely the best of all jobs.

And I was most taken by the intimate—I know no other word to describe it—relationship our neighbors had with their cows, a relationship I soon developed myself. For being among cows, feeding

A time before humans were invented

and milking them every day, caring for their calves, arranging their marriages, sending them to their deaths, and simply enjoying their presence, makes being a dairy farmer unlike any other vocation. Life lived in such intimate contact with the land, and especially with animals, is as ancient a way of being as any that modern people can aspire to.

And, it turns out, it can be a rather profitable way of life as well— well, some of the time.

It has been more than thirty-five years since I was a dairy farmer, but my love and respect for this way of life and my great interest in the people who live it have remained strong. So, like many others, I followed with anxiety the stories of farm failures in the late 1970s and 1980s, the auctions of small herds, and the abandonment of our iconic red barns. I heard, and shared, concerns about "factory farming" and the spurning of the pastures our cows had so loved. I especially feared the loss of the virtues of the yeoman farmer I had so admired—virtues based, I believed, on the ability to farm his own land and to milk his own cows with only his children and his bachelor brother to help him. I worried that the craft of the dairyman was being replaced by "scientific management." I wondered what would happen to the moral fabric of our state when guys with milk on their boots were replaced with guys with ink on their fingers.

But I'm a historian, so I know that time waits for no red barn. After all, what we take as the ancient landscape of our Dairyland was created no more than 160 years ago by people who repudiated the past. I know too that the progressive spirit in Wisconsin re-creates continually with no sentimental attachment to Eden. The Wisconsin Idea itself was born to create prosperity for working people in the present *and the future.*

So in 2006, with a commission from the Wisconsin Milk Marketing Board to produce a series of audio stories, I set out to spend time among cows and dairy farmers again, to talk with them about how dairy farming has changed, and how it hasn't. Not to give too much away, all their boots still had milk, mud, and manure

The Yeoman Farmer

The "yeoman farmer" is the model of the independent American—the tiller of the soil who is beholden to no one but himself. He farms his own land with his own hands and stands ready to abandon his plow to defend his liberties.

The yeoman archers of the late Middle Ages with their longbows are said to have defeated the ancient feudal regime as they loosed their homespun arrows against wave after wave of the mounted French nobility. The yeoman stands his ground because it is his ground.

Thomas Jefferson built his vision of the American Democratic Man on the yeoman farmer. Jefferson was convinced that men who worked their own land must form

Thomas Jefferson's model Americans—the Crave brothers, tillers of the soil

the moral and economic spine of the new nation. Independence and farming would make the real American nobility and guarantee its freedom and prosperity.

---

on them. In fact, I discovered that our modern dairy farmers have found some wonderful new ways to keep themselves on the land and to keep the business of cows a prosperous one.

As I put each of these stories together I was searching for ways to place them in a kind of "deeper soil," a context or understanding that would examine not only *what* something was—a silo, for example— but also *why* it was, what problem it had solved and what changes it had wrought. I came to realize that *the past* is that deeper soil, that things planted in the past of Wisconsin dairying have grown into our landscape of today and our way of life.

This book begins with a brief history of how and especially why Wisconsin farmers learned to care for cows. Understanding these remarkable beginnings—the "big bang" of dairying in our state—explains much about who we are today.

Following this history of dairy time are profiles of contemporary Wisconsin dairy farmers and cheesemakers. These men and women are the heart of the book of Dairyland, people interested in telling me about their love of cows, the land, and the work because they knew I would be telling you. These folks wanted you to know why they love being dairy farmers in Wisconsin.

Because there is great diversity in Dairyland and among its people, each of these profiles is different. They include large and small farm operations, old and new methods. But there also are deep similarities among these farmers. They all care—very well—for their cows. They all care—very well—for their land. They are all most proud to be dairy farmers. Many share the progressive's faith. And they all grin like the Cheshire cat at their good fortune to be dairy farmers in Wisconsin.

Photo by Mark Fay

Dairy farmers like Dennis Iverson would like you to know about them and how they care for their land and their cows.

Unfortunately, there are two things I could not include in this book: the smells that are the real stuff of dairying, and the music of the farm. I could wax rhapsodic about the wonderful way so-called odors make dairying joyfully earthy and strongly existential, or try to help you "read" the music of lowing cows, but I will forgo these pleasures. You must experience them for yourself!

Before I begin I want you to understand that while the stories I will tell you are true, they are not all the truth there is to tell. There are myriad more stories that make up the book of Dairyland, more voices to listen to, new stories continually emerging. Anyway, I do not want to tell you everything, so you will

What We've Got Here

I knew a farmer named Cliff Kronig in Richland County. He was one of the outstanding progressive farmers in the area and a successful dairyman. While visiting with him one day I watched as his sons unloaded wagons full of excellent hay into his barn full of excellent cows. I said, "Cliff, as smart as you are, as hardworking as you are, you could go down to Chicago and make a lot of money."

He looked at me and said, "Yeah, but I could never buy what I've got here."

---

go out on your own and stand at the fence talking cows with your dairy farmer neighbors.

And let me also confess my own considerable biases, because they have influenced the story I will be telling:

I am somewhat of a progressive, and while I love the past, I prefer to live in the present. Besides, I'm pretty sure that the past is not all it is cracked up to be, and the present is not as bad as it seems. Progress has brought, well, progress, and I say that is good.

I believe that *profit* is not a four-letter word.

And I hold that dairy farming is a moral profession, because every dairy farmer I know understands his or her obligation to care well for living things and for the soil that supports them. But of course, at least under the current arrangement, we first must take care of ourselves. That's okay with me. It is possible, I believe, for farmers to care well and even lovingly for their cows *and* make use of them for their own prosperity and happiness.

Now, the first chapter in the book of Dairyland.

14. Milking Time, Good Friends
in Wisconsin.
(Scenes along the country roads.)

Part 1

The Wisconsin Idea of Dairying

A Brief History

THIS MUCH AT LEAST IS CERTAIN: that with the years the Kingdom of the Cow is a constantly widening empire. . . . To some one-time fertile regions she comes late, but she comes to save. When the soil-miner has wrought his perfect work and the earth no longer gives her increase . . . the cow comes to the rescue. From the beginning she has exemplified the doctrine of soil conservation. Where she makes the land her own, green carpets of pasture possess the fields, alfalfa throws its perfume to the breeze and corn waves and rustles in the sunshine. There great new barns rise in place of the old, and white-walled farmsteads speak of peace and plenty. There contented farm folk found dynasties by striking the roots of their lives deep into the soil.

—Jared Van Wagenen, *The Cow,* 1922

The Gospel of the Cow

⟳

THE STORY OF DAIRYING in Wisconsin is the story of how our very landscape and way of life were created. Wisconsin as we know it today is the result of bringing humans and cows together. By making cows the center of our farm life and learning how to care for them, our forebears launched a revolution that changed much more than the way farmers earned their livings—it changed *us*.

Certainly our physical landscape, with its deeply satisfying iconic farmsteads and fields of green plenty, was shaped by cows and how we have learned to care for them. Likewise, it is obvious that the work of the cow and her human partners has brought

This picture from an early issue of *Hoard's Dairyman* was part of the effort by progressives to get farmers to make an emotional and spiritual connection to cows. Cows, this picture says, will reward you with contentment, if you will adopt them into your lives.

"THOSE KINE THAT IN LUSH PASTURES FEED AND LIE DOWN TO COMFORT AND CONTENTMENT."

Hoard's Dairyman, September 13, 1912

great wealth to our state. By learning to make cows "pay," farmers have been able to stay on the land and prosper—no small accomplishment, given the great nineteenth-century rush to the West and the twentieth-century rush to the city. Care of the cow has permitted families to stay together on farms and has preserved a bucolic reality for all of us.

By enriching our soil with her prodigious manure and her beloved grass, cows saved our land, inspired our conservation ethic, and created our great system of sustainable agriculture.

And when our state was in grave danger of having to live with the dire consequences of the profligate squandering of its resources, labor, capital, and economic virtue in the early years after statehood, the cow became a great teacher of economics. For the dairy revolution was a get-rich-*slowly* scheme, an antidote to the economics of exploitation, land speculation, and eventual despair of the early agriculture of wheat in Wisconsin.

As they transformed our land and our wealth, our cows also transformed us, forging our character in part by the moral and work ethic their care demands.

Cows require kindness, routine and predictability, and long-term investments for their well-being and our profit. Dairy farmers must be dedicated to caring well for other living beings and for the resources that feed them. This devotion is the basis of a dairy farmer's business and of our conservation ethic, and over the years thousands of young men and women have carried this ethic off the farm and into the professions, cities, and politics of our state. This ethic of caring is a pervasive influence in our lives. Cows have shaped us.

© Wisconsin Milk Marketing Board, Inc.

This scene speaks to us deeply of prosperity and satisfaction. But it has not always been so. It is the result of a remarkable effort of intelligence, belief, and labor that began 160 years ago—and it is a story still being told.

None of the great transformations brought about by bringing cows and people together happened because the "forces of history" had ordained it should be so. Like our great American Revolution itself, the revolution that made dairying a foundation of Wisconsin life was brought about by men and women who believed in the simple idea that humankind can direct its own fate as long as it acts with inherent human dignity and intelligence.

In fact, the dairy revolution was part of the greater American Revolution, wherein people were freed to pursue their own interests. Dairying succeeded so completely in Wisconsin because it was about earning profit, gaining dignity, and pursuing happiness—and because it unleashed the intelligence of democratic man. Economic historian Eric Lampard called this the Wisconsin Idea of Dairying.

That idea—that intelligence, profit, and rectitude would redeem a fallen agriculture and lift up farmers from mindless toil—was the gospel of dairying preached by some remarkable men and women who established, as they themselves put it, the Church of the Cow. These self-described missionaries, mostly immigrants from New York, were heartbroken by the failure of the American idea of the yeoman farmer to fulfill his Jeffersonian promise. In short, they were horrified by the profligate culture of wheat that was spiraling Wisconsin into despair, emigration, and bankruptcy in the years after the Civil War.

The Wisconsin Idea they proposed was the creation of a new agriculture for a new kind of human being, the yeoman farmer-entrepreneur-intellectual: an intelligent, thoughtful, educated, and diligent professional *agriculturalist*. The cow and her care, and the profits to be made from her, would usher the "hayseed" of those times into the modern world of middle-class comfort, refinement, and self-fulfillment. The gospel of the cow was the good news that, by centering their lives around the cow and her needs, people would prosper on the land. Happily, it proved to be true. Care of the cow surely has brought prosperity to Wisconsin and countless of our farmers.

Why there are cows in Wisconsin, how farmers learned to care for them, and how cows have paid dairy farmers back for their efforts is the story we are about to tell.

The Wheat Error

IN THE 1840s Wisconsin was the West, the next great virgin place for restless Americans to exploit. And exploit they would. At first the pioneers came to make a home and a modest living from the land. Then as they cleared the land and created fields, there began what economic historian Eric Lampard called "settlement by agriculture." Then came the monoculture of King Wheat.

Many pioneer farmers from the East soon lost interest in the self-sufficiency that came from a little corn, a garden, some hogs, a few chickens, and a cow; they wanted money. At first, of course, the soil was new, and quickly farmers took to growing bountiful crops for export and cash, mostly exporting wheat to England and its rapidly growing urban hungry. By 1860 Wisconsin would be first among the states in wheat production, harvesting close to 29 million bushels.[1]

The early agriculture of settlement gave way to the agriculture of unsettlement, you might say, as the fever to make money quickly through land speculation took hold. Farmland was in great demand because of years of high wheat prices, especially as a result of new rail lines to eastern ports. Speculators and farmers—often one and the same—flipped farms for quick profits, and land costs soared as a result. As historian Joseph Schafer said of wheat, "The evil effect of the wonder crop was to reënkindle the gambling spirit in the Wisconsin farmers."[2] *Wheat* became, as Kenosha farmer Philander Judson noted in 1851, "the talismanic word," promising prosperity.[3]

In short: wheat made men a bit crazy. It made some farmers crazy enough to "rob the soil" of its fertility by being "wheat miners" rather than good farmers. By the late 1850s the wheat error was being recognized by religious and agricultural leaders who fretted that Wisconsin agriculture was headed for abject failure. And they worried that the new Western farmer ran the grave moral risk of substituting wild dreams of wealth for stolid Yankee

Wheat became the "talismanic word"—the magic seed that would make farmers prosperous. And for a while it did. Then it nearly destroyed them. But wheat taught Wisconsin farmers the fundamental lesson that profits come only through investment, not exploitation.

responsibility. Instead of land speculation, what was needed, according to the Wisconsin State Agricultural Society, was the building and maintenance of a good farm, "the labor of a life of well directed and well spent industry."[4]

Eventually nature itself took to punishing the wheat-besotted Western farmer, and wheat would prove its own demise. After holding fairly steady throughout the 1870s, Wisconsin's wheat yields began spiraling downward as the land became less and less fertile. Blinded by wheat fever, many farmers paid more for land than they could support by the profits to be made on it.

Then the headlong descent toward agricultural failure was hastened by a visitation of near-biblical proportions. The chinch

"The alarm cannot be too loudly sounded in the ears of western farmers, to beware of plundering the future, for the sake of present advantage too dearly purchased."

—Dr. A. I. Bennett of Beloit, *Transactions of the Wisconsin State Agricultural Society*, 1860

bug came in waves, destroying wheat, livelihood, and hope throughout the Middle West. "Westward ho" became something of a new state motto as native-born Americans abandoned their farms in great numbers for the virgin wheat lands of western Minnesota and the Dakotas.

These were hard times, as W. A. Titus's reminiscence of his childhood on a Fond du Lac County farm in the 1880s helps us understand:

> My years on the farm come back as memories of the hardest kind of work under the most unfavorable conditions and with extremely meager returns. . . . During the earlier period of this farm experience, considerable wheat was grown, and the binding was all done by hand. Some seasons the chinch bugs invaded the wheat fields and sucked the sap from the ripening grain until the straw became harsh and brittle. To bind the sheaves with straw bands at such times meant lacerated fingers. In the morning when the torn flesh was dried and partially healed, the pain from opening up the old wounds was almost maddening. . . . A time came later when bugs and soil exhaustion made it impossible to raise wheat. The farmers were in despair; wheat had always been the cash crop and inability to raise it seemed like a catastrophe.[5]

Wheat farming had left severe deficits in the soil and in farmers' moral core. Animals and grass would rebuild the land and make farmers intelligent, which would make them good. Or so hoped the agricultural, religious, and social reformers.

The Salvation of the Soil

THOSE REFORMERS BELIEVED that livestock was to be the answer to the deficits created by wheat farming. Manure and grass would renew the soil, growing herds would create wealth for farmers, and investments in land, buildings, fences, and herds would restore the idea of building for the future.

The aftermath of the wheat crisis ushered in a decades-long period of experimentation known as diversified farming, during which sheep and cows (raised to provide both beef and milk) were fed mostly on grass. At first animals were fed on unimproved meadows. But in short order the "tame grass" or "better grass" movement transformed wheat lands into pasture and hay lands. (Between 1849 and 1879 the state's hay crop increased nearly sevenfold.)[6]

Many farmers added hogs and chickens to this mix, allowing them to forage on woodlands and providing them some grain, as corn was beginning to be cultivated with enthusiasm in Wisconsin. (The state's corn crop of 1849 was nearly two million bushels; thirty years later it was over thirty-four million bushels.)[7]

In a sense, Wisconsin farmers were auditioning different animals for the role of agricultural savior. For a time sheep were getting the most votes. Unlike dairy cows, sheep require very little labor or capital, both of which were in short supply in the Middle West. The daily demands of the cow for attention—her need for good housing and large quantities of good feed required to produce milk—and her association with woman's work made a commitment to dairy farming a decidedly

Successful Farming, March 1913

Your Soil is Alive

Some years ago a popular book examined "How the Irish Saved Civilization." You might say that manure was the "poop that saved Wisconsin."

second choice. Besides, soldiers needed wool for their uniforms—from 1860 to 1865 Wisconsin's output of wool rose from one million to four million pounds.[8]

The milk cow of the pioneer days was something of a poor relation. She lived on her own, grazing scrub lands and surviving the winter with only the roughest marsh hay to eat. If she had cover from the cold, heat, or flies, she found it herself. The dairy "operation" was at best a branch of family feeding, supervised by the womenfolk and offering a good supplement to children's diets and a bit of fat during the winter. (As the pioneers said, "If you have a cow you can raise a family.") The manure from the family cow was unappreciated and uncollected, making no contribution to the fertility of depleted soils.

Despite dairy cows' marginal status, the fact that on some farms they produced more milk than the family could use was not ignored for long. While there was no dairy *industry* as yet in Wisconsin, some farmers, and especially farmwives, began to accumulate more milk than they needed for home use.

NATURAL MEADOW

Wisconsin, the Great Dairy State, 1914

As wheat gave way to husbandry in the years following the Civil War, Wisconsin farmers discovered one of the state's most overlooked resources: grass. Grass was to be the very foundation of the state's new wealth. Our landscape was beginning to be created.

Before the advent of organized commercial dairying in the decades preceding and just following the Civil War, farm butter and cheese became a means of exchange between farm women and the general store in town. Butter bought buttons, thread, and an occasional bonnet. Generally the butter taken in trade was of poor quality, accepted by the merchant at a steep discount because without it there might be no notions at all purchased from his store. Itinerant buyers would come along at the end of the summer to purchase "Wisconsin wheel grease" for shipment to England.

While the home manufacture of butter for trade allowed surplus milk to be converted into goods, it also greatly added to the farmwife's already burdensome toil. Her eventual liberation "from the dairy" would become one of the planks in the woman's movement from drudgery to homemaking.

The general store was the first market for dairy produce.

From Cottage to Factory

꜀ꛂ

IN 1837 CHARLES ROCKWELL started what was possibly the state's first "retail" cheese venture, selling cheese made on his farm near Fort Atkinson. Around the same time, near Lake Mills the Pickett family started making cheese from the milk of their own cows and ten they rented from neighbors; by 1841 they were milking thirty cows at their early "co-op."[9]

Still, most pioneer farmers at this time continued to consume their milk and dairy produce at home. But a small number of farmers, mostly immigrants from New York cheese country, were beginning to experiment with dairying on a larger scale, expanding their home manufacturing to include cows or milk acquired from neighbors.

New Yorkers were the chief disciples of dairying, having seen the transformative work of the cow back home after the demise of wheat in the East decades earlier. New York cheese was beginning to feed the East's growing appetite for protein that could be stored, and New York dairy farmers were thriving as a result.

But it was not until after the Civil War that a concerted effort to produce and sell cheese commercially was mounted in Wisconsin. Stephen Favill, who hailed from Herkimer County, New York, had built a cheese factory near Lake Mills in the 1840s. After the war Favill retuned to cheesemaking. He would go on to become one of the state's leading dairymen and a tireless advocate for the factory system of cheese manufacturing. Favill and Hiram Smith of Fond du Lac County were among the state's first factorymen, operating independent of farming, buying milk from their neighbors, and looking to profit by converting it through an industrial process that relied on professional expertise and high standards of quality.

Entrepreneurs like Smith, Favill, and the other upright Yankee champions of righteous milk and cheese would be the linchpins in

the Wisconsin dairy revolution. They would lead the way by creating desirable cheese of consistent quality and by preaching, teaching, and regulating their sometimes-irresponsible brethren into industrial rectitude and profits.

Seeing that the market was beginning to reward cheese with cash money was the incentive farmers needed to consider changing their lives completely to care for cows.

The pieces were beginning to fall into place for the ascendancy of the cow and the new type of farmer willing to care for her. By the last quarter of the century, the dairy revolution was well under way.

Purportedly the creamery at Favill Grove, Jefferson County. Stephen Favill was likely one of the first factorymen—cheese capitalists—who transformed milk into money for his neighbors. He was certainly one of the genuine heroes of the dairy industry in Wisconsin, serving as president of the Wisconsin Dairymen's Association in 1880.

The Sorry State of Cheese, the "Band of Missionaries," and the Birth of the Dairy Interest in Wisconsin

Addressing the Wisconsin Dairymen's Association's seventh annual convention in January 1879, future progressive governor W. D. Hoard recounted the short history of this most Yankee of organizations:

It first originated in a resolution offered by the writer in the Jefferson County Dairymen's Association, January 26, 1872. By vote of that association, he was directed to issue a call for a meeting of dairymen to be held at the Lindon House, Watertown, February 15, 1872. . . . The distinctive necessity which was urged at that meeting for such organization, was the low condition of the market, the unmarketable character of the principal portion of our cheese, and the lack of action on the part of buyers to handle our goods. . . .

The price had fallen that season so that good August and September cheese sold for seven and eight cents a pound. . . . In the east [i.e., New York] the business was at the height of its prosperity. With a view of correcting this state of things this band of missionaries went forth. . . . They said that the difficulty with our cheese was, that altogether too few people wanted it. We must have more customers.[1]

The WDA was started in order to improve the sorry state of Wisconsin cheese. Its founders believed a strong dairy industry would create a growing economy, reversing the decline brought on by the wheat failure. Like so many who built our nation, they were civic boosters, encouraging economic growth by capitalizing on and promoting the strengths of their local environment and resources. Not coincidentally, of course, boosters seek to improve their own net worth along with that of their neighbors. This sort of boosterism was one of the great economic engines that built America and Wisconsin.

In order for the WDA to find markets for the state's fledgling cheese industry, it first had to improve the quality and desirability of Wisconsin cheese and lift milk up from its low and often adulterated state. As Hoard noted, "There was no uniformity in the style and quality of our goods, and hence no buyers."[2]

Ultimately, the association had to protect dairying from human nature—that is, from the treachery and sloth of those cheesemakers, companies, and farmers who placed self-interest above the interests of dairying as a whole. H. C. Drake, addressing the WDA at its third convention in 1875, said, "Men as a general rule do not like to look at themselves. We do not like to expose even to our own view the weeds and thistles growing in our mental and moral structure. . . . We had rather cultivate the earth's surface than the hidden recesses of our own nature. . . . Success in any one given direction lies only through a skillful battling with those powerful selfish influences which surround us."[3]

To cultivate human nature and battle selfishness, the association, and other like-minded progressive "interests," would expound a new role for government in Wisconsin. They would help build the progressive state to correct and improve nature, especially its human variety. Regulation, education, and the uplifting of markets would save the dairy industry from numerous threats to the integrity of its products and profits. By the time of Hoard's speech in 1879, he could boast, "Wisconsin stands to-day as the second dairy state of the Union. Have we not a right to feel an honest pride in the result?"[4]

By 1889 the dairy interest had convinced the state to appoint a dairy commissioner to stand sentinel against threats—external and internal—to the quality and profitability of Wisconsin dairy products. In 1888 Hoard himself was elected governor, having run as the "cow candidate."[5] The dairy interest—and the progressive spirit it embodied—was ascending. And to this day dairying is a force to be reckoned with in Wisconsin politics.

1. W. D. Hoard, "The History of the Dairy Interest in Wisconsin," in *Seventh Annual Report of the Wisconsin Dairymen's Association . . .*, comp. D. W. Curtis (Madison: David Atwood, 1879), 128–29.

2. Ibid., 129.

3. H. C. Drake, "The Essential Elements of a Good Dairyman," in *Third Annual Report of the Wisconsin Dairymen's Association . . .* (Fort Atkinson, WI: W. D. Hoard, 1875), 26.

4. Hoard, "History of the Dairy Interest," 129.

5. Eric E. Lampard, *The Rise of the Dairy Industry in Wisconsin: A Study in Agricultural Change, 1820–1920* (Madison: State Historical Society of Wisconsin, 1963), 250.

The Good News of the Cow

⌇

LIKE ANY TRUE REVOLUTION, the dairy revolution was both economic and ideological, calling for reform of hearts, minds, laws, and work. Perhaps the most important of the dairy revolutionaries was William Dempster Hoard, a sometimes preacher and singing master who came to Wisconsin from New York State in 1859. Like his idol, Abraham Lincoln, Hoard had a strong biblical and prophetic streak, leavened with a sardonic wit. Hoard was also an optimist. He became the greatest advocate for salvation by cow.

W. D. Hoard (left) and Belle Atkinson. Hoard built something of an empire on the ascendancy of the dairy cow. His *Hoard's Dairyman*, still published in Fort Atkinson by his descendants, is the leading voice of progressive dairying.

Having returned to Wisconsin after the Civil War, Hoard eventually settled in Fort Atkinson in Jefferson County and in 1870 began his career as a newspaperman—and scold against the ignorance of farmers. "One reason," Hoard wrote in 1889 in his *Jefferson County Union*, "why there is so much truth in the oft-reiterated remark—'Farming Don't Pay'— is that there is not another business on the face of the earth that, in proportion to the numbers engaged in it, supports so many incompetents."[10] To Hoard and the other Yankee founders, the fault for the downward-spiraling moral and economic conditions of the West lay not with nature but with men—especially with men deeply committed to the past.

Hoard and other authors of what would eventually be known as the Wisconsin Idea were men of the Enlightenment, for

The great dairy revolution grew from humble beginnings. But eventually the cow and people willing to care for her would come to define Wisconsin.

whom humans were, if not perfectible, at least improvable, if only they would use their minds.

Hoard and the other dairy founders would propound a program for the improvement of farmers that was the embodiment of the emerging progressive spirit of the time, a spirit born of faith in human intelligence and the social order rationality would create. From this ideology grew a practical program for the wide-ranging improvement of farming practices, attitudes, and education—the beginning of the Wisconsin Idea of Dairying.

Successful Farming, June 1913

SUCCESSFUL FARMING
MUST IMPROVE HUMAN BREED

Mankind itself was the target for Hoard and the other dairy prophets' plan of improvement.

The Progressive Faith and Its Practical Program: The Wisconsin Idea

Wisconsin progressivism has its roots in the European Enlightenment of the eighteenth century. At its deepest level, progressivism is about science and the faith that well-ordered minds, working to uncover what is true and putting that truth into practice, will make life better for humanity.

The Enlightenment repudiated the past and the ignorance that bound mankind to the idea that just because we do it this way, this is the way it must be. The past, said thinkers of the Enlightenment, was already dead. Tradition was too often a myth perpetuated by an ancient regime pleased to give men spiritual stories while enslaving them as beasts of burden to soil from which they could little benefit.

These ideas inspired the minds and passions of people throughout Europe and America. The American Declaration of Independence and Constitution are perhaps the finest testimony to the Enlightenment and the revolution in human society it created. In 1789, fired by the idea that men could be free from the myths of the past and enslavement to rural mindlessness, the citizens of France rebelled against the traditional authority of the monarch, sending much of Europe into turmoil. Success was short-lived, however.

Finding themselves back under the rule of a monarch in 1848, the French again exploded in rebellion. That great conflagration ignited revolts against the German princes in the same year. While for the most part these efforts failed to remove the crown heads of Middle Europe (but did send freedom-fired exiles to America, and especially Wisconsin), the greatest princes, especially those in Prussia and Vienna, realized the Enlightenment was the new world order.

In his 1912 book *The Wisconsin Idea*, state legislative reference librarian and progressive reformer Charles McCarthy used the following fable to extol Prussian social and political enlightenment:

A German prince of the olden time awoke one morning and found that he had no money. He sent for his treasurer, who, in answer to his demand, declared that there was none, that war, robbery, famine and injustice had done their work too well. Alarmed by this reply the prince asked the treasurer what could be done about it, to which he replied: "My lord, we cannot collect taxes unless the farms produce; the farms will not produce unless the farmer works them intelligently; he cannot do that unless he receives a fair profit, protection and an opportunity to live like a man rather than a beast. Give me a portion of the realm; let me keep peace and do justice, and the farmer will produce more and will pay you more taxes." The prince was convinced and gave him what he asked. The treasurer drove out the cheating rascals who had acted as judges; he punished the drunken soldier; he protected the weak against the strong; he imprisoned the usurer and dismissed the tax farmer; he provided markets and exchanges which were honest; he invested heavily in roads and bridges; but best of all he taught the MAN.[1]

Prussian ideas of social progressivism (social security and workers' compensation, for example, were introduced to the world in Prussia) became the model for the program of Wisconsin progressives such as Hoard, McCarthy, and the 48ers, German exiles of the 1848 revolts who settled in Wisconsin. The progressive spirit's true mission was the creation of wealth and the liberation it would bring all people. It would succeed by protecting its citizens from ignorance, injustice, unfettered self-will, disorder, and the tyranny of the past. It would fence off an ever-expanding field in which individual human beings would benefit themselves and each other by an ordered pursuit of profits. It would, in short, create a *common wealth*.

Natural science would be the handmaiden of this economic engine, for it was already making minds freer and lives easier, richer, safer, and happier through its machines, medicines, and democratic rule. And free public education would be the handmaiden of science, preparing rational minds to extend the reach of science into everyday life.

Nature—as discovered by science—would teach mankind. After all, a scientist named Darwin had already uncovered nature's basic operating principle, a principle progressives would put into a program of social and economic improvement.

Progressives built their program of social betterment on the Darwinian principle of selection through competition. Wealth would expand and humans improve because the state would be built upon free, just, and regulated competition, providing a protected space in which selection operated.

This way to human—and dairy cow—improvement was the doctrine of Wisconsin progressives and the dairy interest. And it is still the dairyman's faith today. With the improvement of cows, soil, crops, machinery, markets, and especially men's minds, humanity as a whole will advance. In their hearts progressive dairy

continued . . .

farmers believe that more protein at less cost benefits us all.

Today's dairy men and women are still waging the progressives' crusade against the past and those who think humanity happier there. For progressive dairy farmers, the past is not nearly as wonderful as the future will be. This faith in science, thinking, the future, competition, and a rational plan to extend wealth to all is the Wisconsin Idea.

1. Charles McCarthy, *The Wisconsin Idea* (New York: Macmillan, 1912), 12–13.

The Program for Improved Farming

≫

THE BIG BANG that created dairying in Wisconsin exploded in the decades after the Civil War and continued its inflationary expansion for years afterward as the program for the improvement of farmers was translated into the ever more sophisticated science of the intelligent and diligent care of the dairy cow. It would take many hundreds of progressive farmers, profit-oriented factorymen, university professors, government researchers, and improvement-minded writers to solidify these exploding ideas into a stable universe of successful farming.

Historian Robert Nesbit asked how long it took "Wisconsin's hard-pressed farmers to find salvation—stability and regular profits—with the dairy cow." The answer: "It took a long time, and the acceptance of a discipline that placed many demands upon the prejudices as well as the work habits of our pioneer agriculturalists."[11] These prejudices and challenges were many, but they were perhaps

WHi Image ID 4775

This Oconto farm in 1900 was one of the thousands of places where care of the cow was beginning to be learned. It would take a long time, as historian Robert Nesbit said, for "Wisconsin's hard-pressed farmers to find salvation—stability and regular profits—with the dairy cow." But it had to begin some-where, and this was one of those places.

best expressed in the cry that dairying would "chain farmers to the cow." Unlike wheat cultivation, with its seasonal ebb and flow of labor, care of the cow demands constant vigilance, painstaking attention to detail, and a level of organization that violated the rhythms of living that farmers took to be natural. Besides, men said they were being told to do woman's work, a huge affront to their dignity. Anyway, at this point it was not at all clear how the cow might actually be made to pay.

Looking at the period during which we went from a cow in the bush to a dozen in the barn (roughly, from the 1880s to the 1920s), it is clear that Wisconsin and its farmers had a very long way to go to make the cow profitable. Other than the local trade in homespun butter, there was no market for Wisconsin milk, especially given the haphazard treatment it received from wheat-crazed farmers. It was thought that milk such as this could never make cheese that could compete with the Eastern product.

To make dairying pay, a new, painstaking approach to agriculture called improved farming was needed.

Cows would first and foremost need to be fed on much better stuff than old Bessie had scrounged. And from the beginning of

---

"My neighbors all discouraged me [in 1857 from making cheese], and said I could not make it pay. Capt. Hibbard joined me, and said to me, 'White, you can't do anything here; others have tried and failed.' . . . Whenever I came to town and saw men that knew what I was doing, they would say, 'why don't you fetch me in a piece of cheese,' and made fun of me, because they thought it was not good for anything; but after I got some cured, I took a load to Racine. I went in there a stranger, and put up my team at the barn of a public house. The town was pretty full of Ohio cheese. I went around town until I found one man who wanted some, but he would not buy Wisconsin cheese; it was not good for anything, he said, and it is no use to talk to me."

—W. C. White, address to the Wisconsin Dairymen's Association, January 1879

---

commercial dairy farming, the dairy revolutionaries recognized *grass* as the most important term in the equation of Wisconsin dairy profitability. Grass would create milk. The first step, then, toward the profitable feeding of dairy cows was improving pastures and hay crops by sowing clover and cultivating high-yielding hay fields.

Thomas Pederson, recounting his early life on a Vernon County farm as wheat was dying and dairying was being born, summed up the great hope for the salvation of Wisconsin agriculture through grass and cows.

It looked as if the settlement faced utter ruin. But these Vikings whose ancestors had conquered Scotland, England, and Ireland, and then cut their way through the continent of Europe down to Rome, did not give up. They could not take up the battle against these little insects with their swords and battle-axes but they got together and talked the situation over from every angle. Some way must be found to overcome those little bugs. The idea of moving to some other place did not even occur to them. Finally they decided to change their mode of farming. They had read about a plant called "clover" which was very good feed for cows. Why not try and raise some of this clover and buy cows. They could sell butter at the stores. Up to this time they had not kept cows except to provide their own milk and butter; wheat had been their main crop. This was quite a venture, but something must be done. Remember, this was about sixty years ago [around 1880]. So they secured some clover-seed and sowed it but found that their soil was so depleted by the continual wheat raising that they failed to secure a stand of clover. Because they had no stock, they had no manure, and without manure no clover. Still they did not give up. They pooled their combined credit and secured a carload of commercial fertilizer. Then they raised clover, and cows were bought. They had the chinch bugs licked.

A few years later they erected and commenced operating one of the first coöperative creameries in the northwest. . . .[12]

Cheap Lands in the Clover Belt

Hoard's Dairyman, March 9, 1924

Clover and later alfalfa would change the arithmetic of farming in Wisconsin. Cows and soil would thrive, as would those who fed them on clover.

Cultivated grass was key to profitability for Wisconsin's farmers.

FOR ITS GRASSES WISCONSIN IS DESERVEDLY NOTED

Wisconsin, the Great Dairy State, 1914

The first years during the birth of the new era were heartbreaking. But as more and better cows were accumulated and the new dairy industry came upon a firmer footing, the advance from poverty became more rapid until every farm had as many cows as it could support, and with the cows came hogs to consume the skim milk. The bugs had disappeared so grain could again be raised for feed. New buildings were going up everywhere. The heavy, clumsy homemade shoes were discarded for the much neater store shoe, also the unsightly homemade clothes for the more stylish apparel that could be bought. . . . In short, the poverty stricken settlement had experienced a new birth.[13]

The second requirement of improved farming was manure, the "deposits in the bank of the soil," which cows were pleased to make. By confining cows to barn and barnyard, the new farmer could collect greater and greater quantities of manure and *spread it where he wanted it,* rebuilding and sustaining the soil and fulfilling the promise of livestock farming.

The third term in the new math of dairying was the transformed relationship between humans and cows. Bringing people and cows together in the intimate setting of the barn and barnyard would launch a cascade of hugely important changes—changes in the lives of cows, to be sure, but also fundamental changes in the lives and ethic of farmers. Confining cows to barn and paddock for at least a few hours a day allowed the farmer to observe and get to know his animals, both as a species and as individuals. As J. Q. Emery, Wisconsin's dairy and food commissioner, said in his 1904 address to the Wisconsin Dairymen's Association:

> The business of modern dairying calls forth in multitudinous ways the intellectual activities in the tillage of the soil, the selection, breeding, feeding and rearing of the dairy herd, the manufacturing and marketing of the dairy products that develop a strong, intellectual manhood, and . . . calls into constant activity those kind, considerate, attentive, unselfish acts that cultivate and strengthen the moral nature.[14]

The fourth term in the arithmetic that would add up to dairy profitability was the innovation of winter feeding and the greening

Manure: the engine of sustainability

WHi Image ID 47807

For dairying to succeed, humans and cows would have to build a new and complex relationship in which their daily lives would be intimately entwined. The young woman in this picture is Hannah Iverson (see page 155).

of winter, made possible by the silo. Investing in a silo was a determined step in the direction of dairying as a moneymaking enterprise. Now feed in the form of stored green corn would provide cows with more than fodder; it would give them stuff to milk on. The silo and year-round feeding and milking brought about a cascade of economic and social changes that would transform wheat lands into dairy lands. Silos were visible signals to a farmer's neighbors that he had converted to the new faith of caring for cows.

Finally, if the new farmer—now to be called an *agriculturalist*—was to improve everything, he needed to be taught how; he needed to know a lot more than his father knew. He needed books written for him that would translate the new science of caring for cows into an easy-to-follow program; he needed men of learning to work with

The Greening of Winter

I am experimenting upon an old, run-down farm, which, in 1877, could keep but 6 cows and one horse. I have now in my barn (Dec. 1, 1880) sufficient hay to keep 6 horses, and forage in my silos ample for the sustenance of 40 head of horned cattle, nearly 200 sheep, and 60 swine. I may state also, that, during the past three years, I have bought no hay or manure. This much ensilage has benefited me; and there is no reason why it should not benefit every farmer in like manner. That it may do so, is the earnest wish of my heart.
—John M. Bailey, *The Book of Ensilage; or, The New Dispensation for Farmers*, 1881

Before the adoption of the silo—the first reported upright silo in Wisconsin was built by a Dr. Weeks in Oconomowoc in 1880—cows were milked on the spring flush of grass and survived during the winter on the pathetic dried grass put up as hay. Cows were a burden during the winter, as no milk could be expected for seven months. Before silos, keeping cows did not pay very well.

A silo is basically a pickling jar: a place to preserve corn and other grasses. Unlike hay, which to be safely put up requires most of its moisture and protein to leach on the field, silage preserves these to a greater extent. By dedicating fields to the more intense cultivation of silage crops, keeping animals from marauding over them to feed themselves, and accepting the idea of putting *good-quality* feed up for the winter, farmers began to make the cow pay.

Hiram Smith, that great exponent of commercial dairying, claimed in 1888, "3 cows can be wintered 7 months on one acre producing 16 tons of ensilage, while it required 2 acres of meadow in the same year, 1887, to winter one cow."[1]

With the silo the land yielded more, cows ate much better, and milk flowed year-round. The silo turned Wisconsin's greatest asset, grass, into a full-blown international industry and changed nature's basic operating principle of abundance followed by scarcity. Now, abundance would follow abundance.

By making dairying a full-time occupation, silos kept farmers on their land and gave employment to landless young men eager to get a start in dairy farming. With a now-constant supply of milk, cheese factory owners made new investments in plants and professional development,
continued...

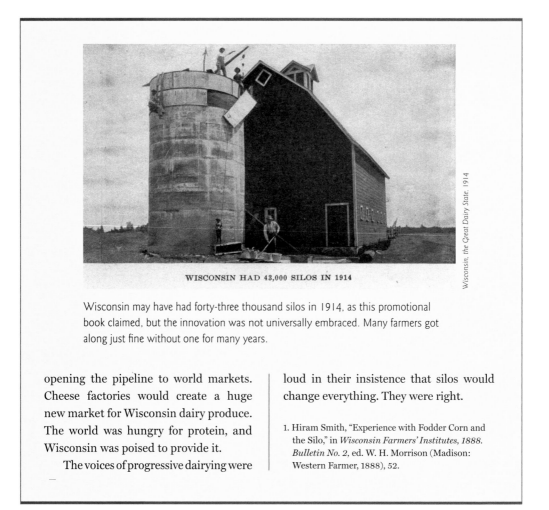

WISCONSIN HAD 43,000 SILOS IN 1914

Wisconsin, the Great Dairy State, 1914

Wisconsin may have had forty-three thousand silos in 1914, as this promotional book claimed, but the innovation was not universally embraced. Many farmers got along just fine without one for many years.

opening the pipeline to world markets. Cheese factories would create a huge new market for Wisconsin dairy produce. The world was hungry for protein, and Wisconsin was poised to provide it.

The voices of progressive dairying were loud in their insistence that silos would change everything. They were right.

1. Hiram Smith, "Experience with Fodder Corn and the Silo," in *Wisconsin Farmers' Institutes, 1888. Bulletin No. 2*, ed. W. H. Morrison (Madison: Western Farmer, 1888), 52.

him in his barn and fields; he needed to be shown, over and over, how "book farming" would profit him (and he needed especially to show his father how that would be so); and he needed a new kind of mentality that would give him the intellectual tools of analysis, objectivity, and experimentation. He needed science in his barn, fields, and mind.

Many American-born farmers, however, derided improved farming as "book- or fancy-farming"—something almost unnatural, an

"With the silo as an aid, milk can be produced on thousands of our farms as cheap in winter as in summer, and prices for this product are very much higher in winter. With all-the-year-round dairying, too, the hired help is kept continuously employed and there is more time to devote to the care and feeding of the herd, there are no flies to annoy the animals and the food supply can be depended upon. . . . Go to the creameries through the country and look up the patrons who supply a uniform quantity of milk month after month through the year and you will find that it is the all-the-year-round dairyman that has the biggest checks and is the most prosperous."

—Clarence B. Lane, *The Business of Dairying*, 1909

affront to their rural authenticity and an assumption of despised city airs. And they wanted little to do with it. At any rate, the new West was opening up, and with it opportunities to continue the agriculture of exploitation.

But while many native-born American farmers rejected the new agriculture of diligence, not so the immigrants from impoverished Europe, who were used to intensive cultivation and unremitting labor. While the leaders of the improvement-through-cows movement were to be primarily Yankee, the foot soldiers included legions of land-grateful immigrants, eager to make dairy farming pay.

Educating the Farmer

᠅

FOR MUCH OF THE NINETEENTH CENTURY, American universities, like their English counterparts, were for the most part places where a small cadre of young men were trained to understand the world Aristotle had described. They were taught to think by reading Cicero and Euclid. And they were taught that the thin air of the abstract was superior to that breathed by men who worked with matter. But American universities would take a decidedly democratic turn by midcentury, turning their backs on the pursuit of pure reason for the pursuit of life-improving actionable science and its practical application—especially to farming.

On July 2, 1862, President Lincoln signed the Morrill Act: "To teach such branches of learning as are related to agriculture and the mechanic arts . . . in order to promote the liberal and practical education of the industrial classes in the several pursuits and professions in life." To fund these institutions for the higher education of practical students, each state was granted thirty thousand acres of federal land for each congressional seat. These "land-grant" universities would turn academia on its head; reason would be placed in the service of democratic human improvement and profits.

In 1887 Congress began similarly funding agricultural experiment stations, and in 1914 the Smith-Lever Act extended the reach of agricultural and domestic improvement to farm and homestead by creating the agriculture extension services at each land-grant school.

Many farmers had their doubts that the tiger would change its academic stripes and actually serve their interests. But William A. Henry, the first dean of the University of Wisconsin's College of Agriculture, slowly began to win over farmers to the idea that science and practical knowledge might be married successfully in Madison. Speaking to farmers in 1884, Henry held out the promise for a new relationship between university and citizen: "I want you all," he said, "to come and see what we are doing; we want to make experiments that will be of use to the people, to find out if we can, a new way or a better way to do things."[15]

With the support of the dairy interests, some farmers began to embrace the marriage of cow and gown. Henry stated unequivocally, "The Wisconsin State Dairymen's Association is the true parent of the Wisconsin College of Agriculture of today."[16]

But by no means were all farmers convinced that higher learning had much to teach them or that the university, a place where intellectuals ruled, could be a real helpmate. And besides, many farmers had no interest in modernizing their farms or their minds. Spending money was not one of the virtues of many early self-sufficient farmers, and debt was out of the question. And why would a fellow want to get fancy ideas about efficiency? Why would he want to imitate his city brother and run a factory rather than a farm?

Nevertheless, Henry and the university made good on their promise to bring useful ideas directly to farmers. In 1885 the regents began the popular Farmers' Institutes "for the instruction of citizens of this state in the various branches of agriculture." A year later the college launched the short course, a twelve-week session held in the winter, during which farmers' sons could live in Madison and study the many branches of farming from the men on the front lines of the modern, intellectual approach to agriculture.

A few years later the first short course for dairymen and cheese- and buttermakers drew young men interested in how science could make their work more profitable.

In the next decades farmers' sons by the thousands would journey to Madison to learn how to think and would return to the farm to employ *ideas* to transform farming into a profession—and make it pay. From this point on it would no longer be necessary to choose between mind and land. Smart young men could exercise their intellects on their fathers' farms (if not with the wholehearted assent of their fathers). Thoughtful farmers would come to define Wisconsin dairymen.

This intellectual approach revolutionized everything. Things that had once been seen as simple, God-given, and whole were taken apart to see how they worked. Whereas at one time cows simply ate grass, gave some milk, and stayed alive, now they were understood to derive nutrients in various proportions from feeds of varying effectiveness. Mankind had invented nutrition, and milk production would skyrocket. Farmers would get the idea—the idea that they could prosper as they learned to feed their cows better, which meant feeding them a balanced, scientific diet.

And by far the most common way dairy farmers learned this was through what may be the most influential dairy book of all time: W. A. Henry's *Feeds and Feeding*, published in 1898. This book became the improved dairying bible, its reference tables of effective feed teaching the way to prosperity.

William A. Henry and his university colleague Stephen M. Babcock were no less than the patron saints of improving dairy farmers and the cheese industry. It is possible to argue that these two men did more to create prosperity in rural Wisconsin than any men before or since.

The road from science to farm was not, however, a one-way street. In 1912 E. L. Luther became the state's first extension agent. People like Luther, educated in science at the university, began to carry the findings of research to farmers and carry farmers' concerns and solutions back to scientists. It is not an exaggeration to say that this dialogue between science and practice improved *everything* for farmers. From fuller stands of clover and better plowing techniques and fertilizer to better feeding, the ag agent delivered the gospel of progress to the farm.

Female county agents also brought farm women their own gospel of progress: the good news that they could now become *home-makers*. For the prosperity of dairy farmers meant living better, and living better meant that women could begin to transform their homes, children, and husbands into expressions of a new ideal, a new way of living comfortable, refined, and educated lives.

Two young men study for their dairy short course around 1920. Exemplars of the Wisconsin Idea, they would return to the farm armed with ideas and a sense of progress. The young man on the right is Edwin Klessig, the grandfather of the farmers at Saxon Homestead Farm in Manitowoc County featured later in this book (see page 61)— a family still employing ideas that make it worthwhile to farm in Wisconsin.

The program of improved farming through systematic good care of the cow and the soil would occupy many of the best minds of Wisconsin for many years. While intellectuals were applying science to the heretofore unexamined practices of farming in order to make the cow pay, others in Wisconsin were busy applying the principles of modern industrial organization and nineteenth-century capitalism to the same question stated in a somewhat different manner: Who exactly would do the paying? Where were the markets for Wisconsin dairy produce? And what did Wisconsin dairy farmers have that anyone wanted?

The Babcock Test

University of Wisconsin College of Agriculture professor Stephen M. Babcock is one of the true patron saints of dairying. His eponymous test for butterfat, introduced in 1890, gave factorymen and dairymen alike real information on the profitable qualities of each cow's milk by assaying its butterfat content. The more butterfat, the more cheese and butter, and thus the greater the profit. Armed with the results of the Babcock test, farmers could begin selecting cows based on the actual yield of their milk and its value in markets. Knowing the value of each individual cow's contribution to profits transformed farmers into business-people, because it showed them that they could use numbers to take improvement into their own hands. By focusing on the productivity of the members of their herds, farmers became active eugenicists, sending the least fit to the butcher. The adoption of number-driven Darwinism was strongly promoted by the forces of progressive dairying. You might say that the Babcock test introduced the scientific method to the barn, replacing farmers' opinions with data.

Besides its inestimable value as a tool for selecting better and better dairy animals, the Babcock test saved the entire factory system of cheesemaking. As one Iowa man said to Hoard, "the Babcock test can beat the Bible in making a man honest."[1] Before the Babcock test, dairy farmers producing valuable milk were paid the same as those whose milk contained less butterfat. (Some farmers were known to add water to their milk, profiting more than the honest dairymen.) The more conscientious dairymen were in revolt, withdrawing their milk from cheese factories and returning to making butter on their own farms. This was a serious challenge to the incipient industry. The Babcock test saved the factory system and with it the market for ever-increasing quantities of milk. Dairy farmers were discovering the profits that improved quality could bring.

1. Hoard repeated this man's words in multiple addresses. See, for example, New York State Dairymen's Association, *Fifteenth Annual Report of the New York State Dairymen's Association* . . . (Utica, NY: Utica Herald, 1892), 205.

Led by the dairy interests, Wisconsin would go on to develop a great industrial system in which dairy producers would more than hold their own in the burgeoning worldwide market for protein. These avatars of modernity would introduce order, system, and science to rural Wisconsin. These virtues of an industrial age

Wisconsin, the Great Dairy State, 1914

A GOOD SAMPLE OF ALSIKE CLOVER

A county ag agent demonstrates a new and better variety of clover. Ag agents like this one translated the findings of science made in Madison to the language of incremental improvement for practical farmers. They were, and are, the great wheels of progressive farming in Wisconsin.

would make rough farmers into careful husbandmen, educated by the cow and the university, converting many—but by no means all—yeoman farmers into yeoman farmer-entrepreneur-intellectuals and transforming a literal cottage industry into a modern, efficient, and profitable world enterprise. Cows would pay farmers because consumers would pay for what would become the best cheese in the world, produced through one of the world's most efficient industrial food systems.

Order, System, Science, and Markets

BUT IF WISCONSIN'S DAIRY LEADERS were to build an industry, they would have to improve each of the rather significant deficiencies of production, manufacturing, and marketing simultaneously. They had little clean milk, little proof that cows could be profitable, almost no good cheese, and certainly no market for that cheese. In short, they had little but grass and manure, eager immigrant farmers desperate for a chance, and the really good idea that intelligence could change everything.

To make dairying work in Wisconsin, the state needed more and higher-producing cows, fed much better than ever in history; more farmers who understood how to care for cows and were willing to do so; milk all year round and roads to transport it; efficient places to convert the milk into cheeses that someone wanted; cheesemakers to operate these factories; capitalists to finance them; and a worldwide reputation for quality. It was a huge undertaking. But progressive men and women set to work.

When Stephen Favill, Hiram Smith, and the other cheese entrepreneurs began pooling their neighbors' milk in those years just after the Civil War, they launched a new system of what was called "associative dairying." That is, they bought and pooled milk from a number of farmers, called patrons, in order to have sufficient quantities to make cheesemaking profitable on a larger scale. This more efficient method of production allowed farmers to offload to experts the rather technically difficult and capital-intensive work of making cheese.

"Now dairying is a variety of farming which teaches a man the absolute necessity of system; for one thing, a dairyman must be a prompt farmer; he is compelled to work to time. . . . Thus the dairyman's farm becomes a school of training in the matter of carefulness. . . . This is what renders his business one of constant exercise for the mind."

—I. J. Clapp of Kenosha, addressing the Wisconsin Dairymen's Association, January 1879

Hoard's Dairyman, February 29, 1924

Knowing the value of each individual cow's contribution to profits transformed farmers into businesspeople, because it showed them that they could use numbers to take improvement into their own hands.

This freed farmers to concentrate on improving farm management and developing better cows, crops, and profits. Specialization was coming to the farm.

Getting milk off the farm and into factories run by experts was to be one of the most important steps in making cows pay. The key to the factory system was the cheese craftsman-entrepreneur-salesman. This professional class of capitalist-craftsmen would teach farmers about their self-interests. They would instruct, cajole, punish, and reward farmers into producing clean milk. That is, they would force farmers to provide milk worthy to be made into cheese and butter that would find favor in the market.

Because meat was relatively cheap, Americans were late in acquiring much interest in cheese. However, by the 1860s, cheese consumption was rising by about thirteen million pounds a year.[17] But it was the export market that would make the cow pay in earnest. The world was hungry for inexpensive protein, and Wisconsin, thanks in part to its grass, was poised to be the world's low-cost producer. The export market for cheese, especially the export of "American" cheese to England, grew eightfold in the decade after the war. (America exported nearly 50 percent of its total cheese produce to England in 1881.)[18] The English demanded consistent, mild, high-quality cheese. But consistently poor quality and the factoryman's treachery would sink the export ship by 1890.

The battle to keep milk as clean and pure as when it left the udder was a long one, but it was essential to the profits and reputation of Wisconsin dairying—and ultimately to the bucolic reality we enjoy today. The battle to make milk safe and pure was one of the most important fought by the industry, by the state of Wisconsin, and by its allies in the world of philanthropy and bacteriology.

From the early years of dairying until the adoption of pasteurization in the early twentieth century and the enactment of stringent testing laws (especially tuberculosis testing of milkers), standards for handling milk were highly suspect and dangerous. Indeed, milk was one of the greatest killers of young children, especially those in the teeming cities. (A federal government study showed, for example, that impure milk supplies were responsible for 195 outbreaks of typhoid, 99 of scarletina and scarlet fever, and 31 of diphtheria from 1865 to 1895.)[19] Cleaning up milk became a crusade for both those concerned with protecting poor children and those working to improve the dairy industry.

From the rough wooden vats of the Klessig family farm cheese factory of around 1880 to the Swiss-neat factories of the late 1920s, cheesemaking left the farm. Our now-iconic and romantic crossroads cheese factories were the cutting edge of industrialization in their time.

Successful Farming, January 1913

The farmwife, keeper of rural wholesomeness, is contrasted with the nasty capitalist in this cartoon. If only farmers were allowed to function in their world of spiritual purity, all would be right! In reality, it was much more complex than that: without capitalists, there would have been no Dairyland.

While cheese was a much safer delivery system than fluid milk, cheesemakers had to wage many wars of their own if they were to raise the quality of their products high enough to win mass consumer acceptance. The Wisconsin Dairymen's Association did battle with retrograde farmers and factorymen who apparently had no interest in seeing milk safer—or in basic human honesty.

Dirty and infected milk could ruin a day's make in the factory, and inferior cheese could ruin the reputation Wisconsin was trying to establish in world markets. In fact, it nearly did.

The first crisis (but not the last) in Wisconsin's bid to become America's Dairyland was known as the filled-cheese crisis. In the late 1880s, English importers discovered that much Wisconsin cheese had been adulterated, with lard or vegetable oil substituted for whole milk. Filling their cheese filled dishonest factorymen's pockets with more than they deserved. So bad did the reputation of Wisconsin's cheese become that honest factorymen took to labeling righteous cheese as Canadian, allowing it to sail to England under a false flag.

Creating good-quality cheese—cheese people would buy—became a major project of the dairy interest and its allies among farmers and politicians. While early progressives did not lose their faith in markets, they came to realize that humans were not going to be redeemed anytime soon and so required a bit of regulating—for their own good. The inspection of dairy processing plants by the state Dairy and Food Commission (created by W. D. Hoard in 1889) and the establishment of a government-managed cheese grading system were elements in the progressives' embrace of regulation and their view that the state should act as the "night watchman" against dishonest people and inferior products.

Increased professional development for makers, state regulations, a number of critical technological advances, and a renewed sense of self-interest would by the 1920s correct the early missteps of the filled-cheese crisis—just in time for the explosive growth of the domestic market.

The Oleo Wars

Perhaps the greatest battle against "dishonest" products was over demon oleomargarine, the golden-colored bête noire of the dairy industry. For years the industry battled mightily against consumers to protect the cream in butter, naturally enlisting the state in this ultimately losing battle. Hoard and legions of state officials and dairy farmers remonstrated in Washington, state capitals, and the national press to demand that milk be given the status of nature's most favored food, resulting in federal margarine taxes, labeling laws, and outright bans.

Wisconsin finally lifted its restrictions on colored margarine in 1967, but the wars to protect the sanctity of milk and make it pure are not over. They are still being fought, for example, against those who demonize fat or argue that commercial milk is not pure enough because it is not "organic." But, for the most part, the dairy industry has triumphed: milk is found on nearly every table in America.

Progressives learned that rules and regulations would aid in the perfecting of farmers. Ensuring clean milk was to everyone's benefit.

NOTICE
For all milk which passes the quality requirements of this factory, as shown by the Methylene Blue Test, the patron will receive a premium of 25 cents a hundred.

W-Hi Image ID 2166

In the last decades of the nineteenth century, Americans began to have more money, immigrants from cheese-producing nations brought with them a taste for cheese, and urban middle classes were acquiring an interest in variety and convenience. Cheese was ascending. By 1900 the domestic market had absorbed all that had been lost in foreign trade as a result of the filled-cheese crisis.

And as farmers began to see their neighbors making a profit with regular milk checks from the cheese factory and butter buyer, and later from the creamery and bottling plant, many began to commit themselves to the cow and her care and the dairying way of life. The idea of growing crops to feed cows and returning those cows' nutrients to the soil appealed to many a parsimonious immigrant farmer. These farmers began to find agricultural sustainability emotionally satisfying—and profitable. And they began to fall in love with their cows and with the idea of dairying.

Becoming Dairyland

ॐ

ATTACHMENT TO LAND AND ANIMALS and an identity as careful husbands of limited resources would become the spiritual and moral sinew of dairying in Wisconsin, often making the difficult economics of commodity farming bearable. These ties, plus an expanding market for milk, would make farming both profitable and emotionally rewarding, fulfilling the promise of the missionaries of dairying: that cows would create a new landscape of prosperity and a new man.

While the anthem of dairying was moving many farmers toward the dairyman's life, most took their time before committing to dairying as their only source of income. While by 1900 just under 92 percent of Wisconsin farmers reported owning some dairy cows, fewer than 15 percent claimed to derive their principal income from dairying.[20] Keeping hogs, chickens, and sheep kept the pioneer ethic of self-sufficiency alive on our dairy farms deep into the twentieth century. Besides, eggs, tobacco, feeder pigs, and sorghum helped pay the mortgage and taxes for quite some time.

While caring for cows was increasingly becoming the way of life for Wisconsin farmers, many would never join the legions of their peers who *believed* in improved dairying (although some of their sons and daughters would). While the agents of progress-through-science-and-order, such as the Wisconsin Dairymen's Association and the university, would create a modern and efficient industry and eventually transform many farmers into astute managers of complex processes, a goodly number never embraced their ethic of modernity. While most dairymen would eventually benefit from efficiency, science, and technology as these became more and more widespread and affordable (and as competition would demand), many farmers preferred a pace more attuned to ancient rather than modern rhythms and a physical relationship to the world—as long as they had some cash left over at the end of the year. And with cash they began finding themselves.

By the late 1910s, the market for milk began an unprecedented expansion, thanks in large part to the efforts of the progressive dairy interests and science to make milk safe, acceptable, and inexpensive to the rising middle class. U.S. milk production increased by 60 percent between 1900 and 1930.[21] And Wisconsin was on the very crest of this great wave of milk going to feed an expanding and wealthier population. The gospel that care of the cow would build a stable rural economy and put money into farmers' pockets year after year was amplified by the growing demand for milk. And Wisconsin farmers heard the news, adding nearly 500,000 cows between 1910 and 1930.[22] Increased demand also increased profits, at least for a while. In 1919 the average price of Wisconsin milk reached a modern-era high of $2.83 per hundred pounds (about $35.60 in modern dollars—Wisconsin dairy farmers today are happy with $17.00 milk).[23] The cow began paying as never before—or since.

By the early 1920s, Wisconsin *was* America's Dairyland, and dairy farming had become Wisconsin's agriculture. Consider:

- According to the 1920 census, more than 90 percent of Wisconsin farmers owned dairy cows.[24]
- Dairy farming itself came to dominate Wisconsin farms by 1923. In that year 55 percent of farm income derived from dairying.[25]
- In 1889 Wisconsin cheese accounted for 26.6 percent of the total cheese produced in the United States. By 1919 more than 63 percent of all cheese made in the United States came from Wisconsin.[26]
- In 1869 Wisconsin had only 54 milk processing plants (all of which were cheese factories). By 1899 it had 2,018, and by 1919 the number of processing plants had climbed to 2,872. Milk had become an industry.[27]

By 1912 Wisconsin had the cheese.

Hoard's Dairyman, October 18, 1912

- The value added to Wisconsin's economic output by these plants increased by an astonishing 434.5 times in the fifty years from 1869 to 1919.[28]
- Between 1909 and 1919 production of cheese went from around 147 million pounds to nearly 299 million pounds, doubling in ten years.[29] By the early 1950s Wisconsin produced more than half a billion pounds of cheese annually, a nearly quadruple growth over 1909.[30]
- By 1923, 70 percent of all cheese produced in the United States was produced in Wisconsin.[31]
- And, by 1923 creamery production of butter exceeded farm-made butter by a factor of 16.[32] Dairy production had left the farm.

In a mere sixty years Wisconsin had risen from a state of economic and moral depletion to become a national icon of wholesomeness and rural rectitude. Men and women had created Dairyland, and the beneficent goodness of cows would define us from then on.

The great success of early-twentieth-century milk producers was that milk became a mass-market commodity. A mass market meant new levels of income; *commodity*, however, meant almost continual difficulties in matching supply with demand and profits with effort and investment. The expanding mass market for milk would unleash the progressives' engine of change: competition for fitness in a world of ever-cheaper milk. This would put strong selective pressure on farmers to find ways to stay on the land. Dairy farmers would experiment with different ways to keep cows paying and themselves enjoying their lives.

Perhaps the most ancient response to the opportunity to make profits from the land is to abuse it, as Wisconsin saw during the wheat craze. By the time of dairying's great expansion, Wisconsin farmers had heard, and to varying degrees taken to heart, the sermons on replenishing the soil's vitality through manure, clover, and alfalfa. Yet in their rush to get more cows on their land and more yield with less work, many farmers took little mind of the runoff that was washing away the world's richest topsoil. But by a most remarkable effort during later decades, the federal government and the

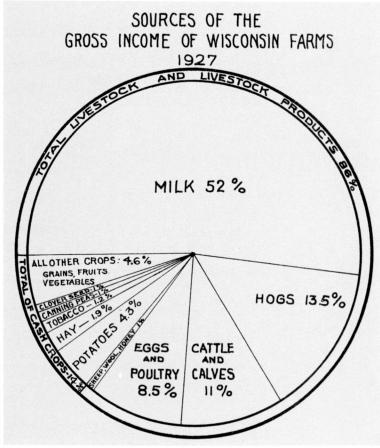

SOURCES OF THE
GROSS INCOME OF WISCONSIN FARMS
1927

TOTAL LIVESTOCK AND LIVESTOCK PRODUCTS 86%

MILK 52%

HOGS 13.5%

ALL OTHER CROPS: 4.6%
GRAINS, FRUITS
VEGETABLES
CLOVER SEED-1%
CANNING PEAS-1.2%
TOBACCO — 1.9%
HAY — 1.9%
POTATOES 4.3%
TOTAL OF CASH CROPS-14%
SHEEP, WOOL, HONEY 1%

EGGS
AND
POULTRY
8.5%

CATTLE
AND
CALVES
11%

university bribed farmers into conserving their soil. With this was born our rural landscape and its deeply satisfying alternating strips of green and gold that so elegantly follow the contours of our land. Today conserving the soil is an article of the dairying faith.

To keep cows paying enough (or even more than enough), many dairy farmers began to take matters into their own hands: they would attempt to control prices by controlling production. For too many farmers and their populist representatives, the difference between what consumers paid and what farmers received for their milk was morally offensive and politically actionable. Farmers were being

Kraft, Pasteurization, and the Mass Market for Cheese

Joseph L. Kraft, on the twentieth anniversary of the founding of the company that bears his name, described the previous sorry state of cheese and its redemption by science and consumer-oriented mass marketing.

In more than twenty years the American cheese industry has risen from disorganization to prosperity. . . . There is no question that [his companies'] methods of manufacture and distribution have been the most beneficial influences in the dairy industry in fifty years. When the companies began operations the industry in this country was composed mostly of small units, insignificant financially and handicapped by lack of capital. As a result there were periodical market fluctuations ruinous to producer, manufacturer and wholesaler.

When milk was plentiful its price fell to unprofitable levels. Manufactured cheese in storage for ripening, an essential process for high-grade cheese, would decline in value to a point where to avoid total loss it had to be thrown on the market.

Cheese made by the old methods was perishable and it could be distributed only in a limited territory.

The discovery of pasteurization marks the turning point in cheese merchandising. It permitted marketing in packages. It gave the consumer unvarying flavor, quality and cleanliness. . . . Meanwhile, extensive advertising created thousands of new consumers. This in turn made it profitable for the farmer to increase his herds.[1]

Kraft was right. His consumer-friendly "high-grade" pasteurized cheese marked a turning point for Wisconsin dairy farmers. In the twenty years following Kraft's innovation, Wisconsin doubled its production of cheese.[2] Science, technology, the profit motive, and mass marketing put many more cows into Wisconsin barns and much more money in our farmers' pockets.

1. "Kraft Recalls Rise of Cheese Industry," *New York Times*, February 26, 1928.
2. Eric E. Lampard, *The Rise of the Dairy Industry in Wisconsin: A Study in Agricultural Change, 1820-1920* (Madison: State Historical Society of Wisconsin, 1963), 453, table E.

robbed, these populists said, by the big capitalist and his lackey, the hated middleman. The producer himself, they argued, must control his own produce and demand *his* price. Farmers must cooperate to control the market.

Animosity between farmer and capitalist runs deep in rural America and its social politics. Many farmers objected on both moral and economic grounds to enriching through their own toil people who did no "honest" work. Farmers often contrasted their own basic nobility as people of sweat and soil with the capitalist who does no *real* work but takes all the profits. To right this inequity, farmers created one of Wisconsin's most important and characteristic social and economic experiments: the cooperative marketing movement that played a greater and greater role in marketing Wisconsin dairy produce during the 1920s and 1930s.

Getting farmers to cooperate to control their own economic fate and to assert their inherent dignity as Brothers of the Grange was the alternative to the progressives' free-market project. Dairy farmer cooperatives would make the cow pay by controlling production to keep prices higher and by sharing the profits made in marketing their own products.

While the farmer cooperative movement never really succeeded in herding farmers into controlling their output, notwithstanding strikes and milk pooling and dumping, it did succeed in putting more money in farmers' pockets by sharing profits from its expanding control of the distribution and marketing of milk. Between 1930 and 1970 the share of milk marketed by farmer co-ops went from 30 percent to more than 70 percent of the total market.[33] Many a farm couple cashed out their co-op stock to retire in comfort.

The pressure on farmers to adapt or die gained force in earnest around the 1930s. Beginning with the Great Depression, many thousands of men and women would abandon dairying, leaving farms for the city, in a great acceleration of the historic migration off the land. In 1900, for example, more than 43 percent of Wisconsin's population were members of farm families. By the mid-1930s there were more than two hundred thousand farms in the state with one

Some dairy farmers sought control over their lives through collective—and sometimes illegal and violent—action, like this demonstration of anger and resolve along a railway line near Burlington in 1936 at the height of the Great Depression. Dumping the milk of farmers who refused to join milk pools was meant to enforce farmer control over prices, much like industrial labor unions' attacks on "scabs." Simply put, many Wisconsin dairy farmers believed capitalists were cheating them by taking the greatest portion of the profits from their milk, squeezing them into penury. Many other dairy farmers stuck to their ideal of yeoman independence. The result was a kind of civil war between progressive and collectivist-minded farmers—a split that still defines Wisconsin agriculture.

million people, nearly one-third of the population, living on them. But by 2000 only around 2.5 percent of the state's population were living on farms.[34]

The number of Wisconsin farms with dairy cows reached its highest point of 180,695 in 1935. By 1999 that number had fallen to 21,624, an eightfold decrease.[35] It is tempting to think of this great migration as a kind of forced march, sending off to the city many thousands of unwilling men and women, the victims of grinding competition, thieving capitalists, and the rapacious demands of the urban masses and their lawmakers for cheap food. Of course, many were forced off their land by the terrible economic conditions of the time, and for these people leaving the farm and the farming way of life was a tragic loss. But for the most part, it was the sons and daughters of farmers who left for the cities, and for them it represented not tragedy but liberation. Going to the city meant the chance to enjoy the fruits of progress and modernity. It meant freedom from constant physical toil, pervasive odors and mud, often-unhappy family dynamics, and the economic travails of commodity production. For many, leaving fathers for whom progress was too expensive and far too socially ostentatious was to be liberated to pursue new ways of doing and living. And for many farmwives and children, a middle-class life with leisure to pursue self-improvement was painfully elusive. Working seven days a week still defined farm life for many, and how much work the family could accomplish every day was the compass of many farmers' self-worth.

It was this loss of free labor and the demand for a middle-class life that would open the barn door to science, technology, mechanization, and profit-driven management practices for an increasing number of Wisconsin dairy farms. Greater milk production would be achieved not through increasing the number of cows

WHi Image ID 76307

We can never know if this boy heard the sirens of the city calling him as he threw down hay this winter day so many years ago. Many boys and girls did, of course, and left. But for many others, the smells of hay, cow, and milk were the stuff of the home of their youth—a place they preferred to remain.

milked or by working harder but by greater efficiencies and working more intelligently.

By the early 1950s, we had begun a great leap forward in fulfilling the progressives' program to transform farmers from people whose backs always hurt into agriculturalists whose minds were fully engaged. Cows had stabilized Wisconsin farmers. Now cows would make them the equals of their city cousins.

The Age of Intensification

꒳

WHILE THE SIZE of the average Wisconsin dairy herd has been steadily increasing since 1920 by slightly more than one-half cow each year, the total number of cows in Wisconsin reached its high-water mark in 1945.[36] Each dairy cow's production of milk also grew during this period. But beginning in the 1950s, the *pace* of each individual cow's production began a great and unprecedented acceleration. Consider:

In 1924, a Wisconsin cow produced on average 5,280 pounds of milk. By 1954 this had increased to 7,100 pounds, an increase of nearly 60 pounds, or slightly more than 1 percent in each of those thirty years. By 1984 each cow gave 12,856 pounds, more than doubling her 1924 ancestors' contribution. These generations of cows increased their contribution by more than 190 pounds, or more than 2.5 percent on average, in each of those thirty years. (While today's cow gives on average 60 percent more milk than her great-great-grandmother of 1984, there has been no growth in the *acceleration* of production.)[37]

At the same time, the price of milk in real terms has fallen. A consumer in 1920 paid about $.67 for a gallon of milk,[38] which would be $7.30 in 2010 dollars. That today's shoppers pay considerably less than $7.30 for a gallon of milk is the triumph of modern dairying's increasing efficiencies. Whether it was a triumph for farmers remains an open question—if farmers' payments had increased at the same pace, they would receive $31.00 per hundredweight rather than the $15.00 or $16.00 they get today.

While children worldwide were benefiting from less and less expensive protein, those farmers who had decided to remain in the business needed help, especially because by the second half of the twentieth century California was adding great new quantities of milk—along with huge doses of competition and downward price pressures on Wisconsin producers.

In the 1950s dairy farmers would begin to get the help they needed. They would, as it were, trade their horses for a Deere and their "craft" knowledge for the fruits of science. And they would begin to give up their I'll-do-it-all-myself ethic for the help of experts and laborers.

Before World War II, according to Wisconsin dairy writer John Oncken, one of agriculture's most important events was the National Corn Picking Contest. In other words, farmers' great source of pride was in what they could do with their hands—and their backs and their horses. After the war this would all change. Changed too would be the balance between the historic self-sufficiency of dairy farmers and their dependency on the world beyond their fence line.

"The most glorious event in my life was [when my father bought] 2-4-D to kill the thistles."

—John Oncken, farmer's son, retired county dairy agent, and dairy journalist (oral history interview, March 2010)

Wisconsin dairy farmers had always bought things like lime, clover seed, horses and bulls, and even milking machines from others. And naturally they had shipped some of their nutrients away in the form of milk. But the inherent parsimony of dairying—its sustainability—has always been among its most appealing characteristics, especially for generations raised to spurn debt and appreciate manure.

But the new mechanical, chemical, sexual, medical, and intellectual sources of power becoming available to farmers from the outside world would transform the dairy farmers' life, health, and status as never before; usher them into a very modern world; help keep them competitive—and create our Dairyland of today.

To this modern, transfigured world, and to the men and women who still earn their livings among cows, we now turn our attention. For the forces, faith, and ideas that shaped our land into our landscape and our farmers into prosperous and deeply responsible citizens have never ceased their work.

From Horses to Deere: New Sources of Power in Dairyland

In the years 1910 to 1914, it took 3.8 person-hours to produce one hundred pounds of milk on U.S. farms. In the years between 1946 and 1949, 2.6 hours were needed. In the period from 1960 to 1961, it required only 1.4 working hours to produce a hundredweight of milk. Thus, in fewer than fifty years American dairy farmers had increased their productivity by more than two and a half times.

In those same fifty years, American farmers reduced the labor necessary to grow one ton of hay from 10.3 hours to 3.3 hours, requiring only one-third the time previously needed. The labor-savings gains to produce one hundred bushels of corn are even more remarkable. In 1960–1961 it required 14 person-hours for 100 bushels. In 1910–1914, this yield had demanded 135 hours, a reduction of labor by more than 9.5 times.[1]

These gains in productivity were possible because dairy farmers began to make a fundamental shift in their ancient habits, abandoning their historic reliance on homegrown sources of power for new, more powerful sources purchased from others. These farm-shaking new sources included much larger and smarter machines, unlimited new fossil energy, human-invented chemical compounds, new genetic potency for animals and crops, much greater sums of money made available in the form of credit, professional expertise, and many new ideas.

For example:

- In 1935 one out of ten American farms had electricity. By 1950 nine out of ten farmers could run milking machines, cool milk to safe temperatures, listen to the radio, and move manure out of barns without lifting a pitchfork or breaking a back. Farmers bought electricity, and their lives and work changed.[2]

- Even up to the 1960s most dairy farmers kept at least one bull to contribute his, and only his, genes to the herd. In the 1950s frozen semen began to make the family bull obsolete, opening the door to a tremendously expanded gene pool for the improvement of cows. Bulls would no longer terrorize farm families. With artificial insemination any farmer could take advantage of the new science of genetics, marshaling the sexual power of the world's greatest bulls to improve the value of his cows. According to Carl Coppock, between 1961 and 1998, 36 percent of the gain in milk production can be credited to gene pool improvement.[3]

- New strains of forage and field crops such as vernal (spring-flowering) alfalfa and
continued ...

continually improving corn and soybean hybrids increased yield many times over. No longer would farmers save seed each year to start their next crops; farmers could now buy much better varieties than they could grow themselves.

- Controlling 285 horses in a plowing team presents what could only be called insurmountable problems. With a 285-horsepower tractor, there is no problem. The revolution in farm mechanization was profound. Consider hay making: it took one person driving the team, two on the wagon, three or four to rake and fork hay onto the wagon, and then two or three to get the darn stuff into the hot and dusty mow. Being able to put up but a few acres a day meant leaving many acres of valuable forage to overmature before it could be brought in. Balers and hay combines changed all that. Cows ate much better as a result, and so did farmers.

- Many farmers took it as a matter of pride to rely on their own knowledge acquired from their fathers and neighbors to manage their crops, land, and cows. Most kept a small notebook in the pocket of their overalls to track the yield of the back forty over the years. As the age of specialization dawned, however, new cadres of professionally trained consultants were available to perform complex scientific analysis of the nutrient components in each acre of land, the nutritional value of each load of feed, the genetic value of each cow, and the health of the herd. Dairy farmers began to purchase intellectual power from off the farm.

- Before chemical weed control, field cultivation consisted of a farmer making pass after pass at very slow speeds up and down rows of corn. This was labor- and fuel-intensive work performed at the expense of making the best possible hay. Many dairy farmers began to appreciate the idea that they could buy a kind of victory over nature's pests without the need to sit on a tractor hour after hour.

Freeing farmers from grinding toil liberated them to use their minds more and more. Many farmers considered this worth paying for.

1. "Crop and Livestock Man-hours Down," *Wisconsin Crop and Livestock Reporter*, July 1963, 30.
2. Carl E. Coppock, "Selected Features of the U.S. Dairy Industry from 1900 to 2000" (address, annual Southwest Nutrition and Management Conference, Phoenix, AZ, February 24–25, 2000), Table 1.
3. Ibid.

In the profiles that follow we are keen to answer many questions.

We will especially want to know the state of the historic promise of dairying in Wisconsin: that men and women can find prosperity, satisfaction, and even happiness by caring for cows. How are today's dairy farmers in Wisconsin still making cows pay?

Are the ancient satisfactions still sufficient, or are dairy people finding new ways to be happy on the land?

How fares the obligation to care kindly for other living beings that dairy farmers adopted so many years ago? Does farmer parsimony still make them careful stewards of our land and resources?

We want to know, perhaps quite selfishly, if our dairy farmers can still serve *us* as embodiments of the sturdy, self-reliant folks that built the economically moral world we have inherited.

And we want to know if dairy farmers are still happy to find themselves at home on the farm. Because our landscape, our identity, and our prosperity still depend on it.

The people we are about to meet are the inheritors of 160 years of history; it is the soil out of which they have grown.

Photo by Mark Fay

PART 2

IN THE COMPANY
OF COWS

CONVERSATIONS WITH
FARMERS AND CHEESEMAKERS

THE FARM IS NOT THE PLACE to become wealthy. . . . Certainly I should not go on the farm with that idea in view. But if I wanted to live a happy life, if I wanted to have at my command independence and the comforts of living, I do not know where I could better find them than on the farm; for those very things which appeal to an educated taste are the things which the farmer does not have to buy,—they are the things which are his already.

—Professor L. H. Bailey in 1898, quoted by Isaac Phillips Roberts in *The Farmstead*

"Germans have this strong feeling for the land. And this was our heritage. Every Sunday we went out into nature. And that was always our delight. I was raised to think nature divine. . . . My husband, Eddie, loved farming. He just loved the land. You just didn't want to have a machine that runs back and forth and exploits the land and not replenish it. Eddie went to the dairy short course and he had Aldo Leopold as a teacher. Believe it or not, Aldo Leopold influenced him a whole lot." —Margaret Klessig

Finding Themselves on the Farm

༜

SAXON HOMESTEAD FARM

*I think of our cows lying in the field at nighttime with the
stars and moon above. And I think of the quietness that they
have. The peace they have in their lives. The cows are out in the
grass chewing their cuds. There's something very affectionate and
peaceful when you look at that scene. There's something deep and
in the center of my heart; it is why I love dairy farming. We're
husbanders of animals and stewards of the land. We're all part
of the animal kingdom, and to treat animals honestly and with
integrity and kindness makes me feel good. I give to them and
they give to me. That's a cardinal commandment, I would
say, of a moral way of living. —Elise Heimerl*

THIS IS THE STORY of how a new generation of farmers have
re-created their family's 160-year-old farm. It is the story of how
they have found themselves by farming in a way that both pleases
and profits them and that keeps them, happily, on the land.

This is the story—only one of the interesting stories—of the
Klessig family's farm, a place on the map since 1850.

Margaret, the current Klessig matriarch, was born into Viennese
society in 1921 as the glory of imperial Europe was dying. Her father
had been a regimental surgeon in the army of the Emperor Franz
Joseph, the last great monarch of the House of Hapsburg. Margaret
was raised with music, poetry, and hikes into the mountains to

Courtesy of the Klessig family

The Klessig farm, probably around the turn of the century. It was already prosperous. The home on the left in this picture is the home Margaret Klessig lives in today.

Twenty-five yards from their barns is a true monument to the family's deep involvement in dairying: their ancient stone cheese factory, perhaps the oldest in Manitowoc County and surely one of its first woman-run businesses. Today the family has a modern cheese factory so they can once again make greater profits from their labors.

Photo by Mark Fay

worship nature divine. She would go on to spend the rest of her life on a Wisconsin dairy farm, happily, with no regrets.

For this farm of her husband, his father and grandfather and great-grandfather (and now her sons, daughter, and grandson) is a place where a love of nature, its moral obligations, and its aesthetic pleasures are mixed with milk, cows, manure, mud, money and debt, and birth and death. For 160 years Klessigs have found sufficient satisfaction, made enough money, raised plenty of children, and kept faith, as best they could, with nature on this farm.

Like nearly every other extant dairy farm in Wisconsin, the Klessig farm has been created and re-created many times. It has been transformed by new technology, new science, new definitions of progress, better ways to sustain the land and animals, new aesthetics, and, most important, new ways to improve the income, living standards, and satisfaction of the men and women who've lived and toiled there.

This generation is no exception, for they are re-creating their inheritance in order to see *their* ideals reflected in their cows, the vitality of their soil, the quality of their own cheese, and the value of the heritage they will pass on to the next generation. They are, in short, trying to create a place they want to be and where they can afford to be.

To create the place they want to be, this family of farmers has revolted—thoughtfully and conservatively—from the idea of intensive dairy farming and what was for a time the true way of the dairyman: the way of their father.

"I have one particularly pleasant remembrance about my place,— that I in a certain sense created it."

—Oliver Wendell Holmes

Today Saxon Homestead Farm (so called because its founder, Johan Andreas Klessig, started a "new old order" of Saxon farmers at this place in 1850) supports three families, one grandmother, and one grandson. This farm belongs to people for whom history and principles matter, people who fiercely adhere to their obligations to the men and women who invested so much of themselves in this place. As Margaret's daughter Elise puts it:

When I take a walk through our little ten-acre woods, my father's ashes are in there, and my Down-syndrome brother's ashes are in the woods. And that to me is a sacred little spot on earth. And we know that Grandpa and my brother Connie can see the cows every day walking by. And they can see the activity on the farm. And we feel that they are still one of us. And so we have kind of a moral obligation to not let them down, to keep things rolling.

However, the strong force to keep family history rolling was met by the very strong forces of economy, personal history, and new aspirations for farmers' lives. The old way-of-the-dairyman, valued for its success, also enchained many souls.

Margaret's husband, the late Eddie Klessig, was by universal acclaim the embodiment of optimism, kindness, and good humor. He was also a nationally known farmer-radical, asserting that nature and just-plain-farmers had a stake in agriculture.

Eddie Klessig inherited a prosperous farm from his father and set about to keep it modern as was the family's practice and economic necessity. Embracing the gospel of improved farming, he built the farm into a model of progressive dairying. Eddie kept his cows mostly confined in a tie-stanchion barn, the better to feed them for optimal production and to collect their manure. He used his green fields to make hay and silage, which he fed year-round to his cows along with acres of field corn. He built one of those blue Harvestore silos that were the cutting edge of dairying thirty years ago. (In their day, Harvestore silos were a sort of flag of progressivism, flown proudly by improving dairypeople. They were statements of prosperity and symbols of status. And, all too often, they were black flags of debt. The younger generation of Klessigs recently deconstructed their Harvestore, giving it "to a guy to take away.")

"When I was in high school, we were a conventional dairy where all the cows were locked in a barn. We handled a lot of manure and feed by hand. It was a difficult way for a youngster to gain an appreciation for farming. Because it seemed we were always in shit."

—Robert Klessig

WHi Image ID 76305

While cow manure has been one of the saving graces of Wisconsin's soil and economy, it requires a rather deep involvement that permeates much of the life of a farmer. Many young people who grow up on dairy farms wish to leave the pervasiveness of manure behind. (The man in this picture is unidentified.)

Eddie Klessig used the approved crop rotations of the time, taking seriously his obligation to soil fertility and conservation. To prosper he sprayed herbicides and applied chemical fertilizers. Diesel fueled his operation. He was a very good dairyman, and he prospered—at least some of the time.

But keeping up with change in agriculture is expensive, often pushing the most frugal farmer into debt, worry, and exhaustion. In addition, farmers needed to solve the basic problem of family farming: how to keep the family together and find room for two or even three growing families on the farm. And for many dairy farm sons and daughters, their parents' way of farming won't satisfy their personal expectations for a life unfettered to the ways of the past stuck in manure.

And yet, today three of Eddie and Margaret's five children farm here, along with a son-in-law and

Hoard's Dairyman, October 25, 1912

THE BOY ON THE FARM.

"Don't drive the boy off the farm. Arrange the farm work so that he will like it."

The proud inhabitant of the new farmer overalls is Eddie Klessig, a boy who grew into a proud farmer. Note the stone silo. It was one of the first built in Wisconsin, and it still stands today because Margaret and her children fought the wrecking ball of progress to preserve it.

a grandson and his wife. So the Klessigs have found a way—a creative and satisfying way—to keep being farmers.

Karl Klessig is fifty-one and was just short of his Ph.D. and a career at the University of Wisconsin in Madison when he returned home twenty years ago to farm with his father and new brother-in-law, Jerry Heimerl. What was it that his parents offered him and his siblings? Here's how he saw it:

A major opportunity that we'd been presented by my father and my mother in the late '70s and early '80s. They had really emphasized through much of my childhood that farming and rural Wisconsin was a phenomenal place to be and a great place to raise a family. And when you connect to the land and the environment around you, it will lead to a very fulfilling life.

I bought that then to some degree. The fact of the matter is that I'm here.

But for the first five to ten years you question whether that was the right decision. Jerry and I farmed through the mid-'80s, when Reaganomics, the trickle-down effect hit us very hard. That was a very tough economic time to be farming. We struggled trying to keep the ship afloat.

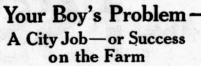
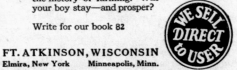
Keeping new generations on the farm has been one of the great conundrums of family farming, as Mrs. D. Huntley cautioned the Wisconsin Dairymen's Association in 1877: "Not that all the children of farmers can be drilled like so many soldiers, to fall into the ranks, and make farming their business; this is in no way desirable; the point to be gained with these children of the farm is, so to conduct their home life that they will not become disgusted with the labors, the responsibilities, the isolation from society, or any of the various conditions to which farmers are subjected; not only this, it should be so conducted that the boys, and the girls as well, may lose none of the benefits arising from country life."[1]

Elise's husband, Jerry Heimerl, is a thoughtful fifty-seven-year-old Vietnam-era veteran, son of a dairy farmer, and partner in Saxon Homestead Farm for nearly thirty years. He is a graduate of the resource management program at the University of Wisconsin at Stevens Point who caught the sustainability bug early:

In the early '80s I started thinking about sustainable agriculture, reading about it and understanding what it was. I did not like using the insecticide we used for corn. First of all, it smelled terrible. Skull and crossbones on it. And the relationship to cancers that was surfacing in the press. And I started thinking, can we go backwards; can we back up and use less?

Elise continues:

This system was breaking my neighbors. And the attrition of what used to be 120,000 farms down to 12,000 farms—yoo-hoo, is anyone listening? That was a bell-ringer when we came home from college and decided, to hell with the chemicals and to hell with the buildings and the machinery. Those are burdens on our neck. We wanted to take all of the intense energy out of our life.

Jerry Heimerl and the great wealth of Wisconsin: alfalfa

Photo by Mark Fay

But the energy needed to keep the wheels of dairy farms going only intensified during the first years after Jerry, Elise, and Karl returned to the farm. Higher productivity was the banner under which so many of our dairy farmers marched to battle against worldwide competition— and with great success, it must be said.

But for many, especially some young dairy farmers, running faster became unsustainable and distinctly un-fun. Costs kept rising and milk prices kept not rising. Finding ways to deintensify dairy farming and make it something that farmers could afford to do began to exercise the minds of dairypeople desperate to stay in farming.

Enter Robert, youngest Klessig and elemental force of nature.

Robert had decided early in his life that being mired in manure was not his idea of the divine in nature. As his mother's family had hiked into the Austrian mountains, Robert decided to take a hike himself, into the wilderness of Alaska, Idaho, and Montana for twelve years. For Robert, a world in which nature dominated man was the place for him. Less intensity, not more, would bring him the happiness that nature offers. Being a wilderness guide in a huge all-surrounding place was preferable to toiling in a confined dairy barn.

The problem was that Robert was really a son of the farm and his much-loved father. He would come back to Wisconsin to farm, he said, if he could return to a place where a more natural balance among human, cow, machine, and nature could be restored.

The solution to his dilemma came into focus out west, where he met the Native American Bovine Spirit itself, the Great Herbivore,

Elise Heimerl, son Joe, and a neighbor during haying season. The rhythms of farming allow for much gabbing with neighbors, a reward for working the land.

Photo by Mark Fay

Robert Klessig

the Ur-Grazer: the American bison (and where he had also seen the success of the less spiritual but more profitable commercial grazing of beef cattle).

Robert returned to Wisconsin in 1988 to find Jerry and Karl struggling to keep the farm going financially. Farmers were looking for ways to be more efficient and less driven by the need for more machinery, energy, and capital. According to Karl:

When Robert came back in 1988, he said, "Guys, you've got to do something different." He said, "You know, I love farming, but I really don't want to do what you're doing—which is driving tractors, planting corn, milking three times a day."

He said, "I really think we should graze." And lo and behold, Jerry was already being introduced to [grazing] from farmers in the state. And the sustainable ag movement was starting to gain a foothold for many dairy farmers.

The foothold of grazing on Saxon Homestead Farm began with the footfalls of bison. Buffalo would mentor Heimerl and the Klessigs on the finer points of the conversion of grass into milk checks. As Robert puts it:

Raising American bison taught me more about grass production and grazing than anything else. It was kind of interesting to lie down in the middle of a paddock with one hundred big herbivores munching around you. And sneaking a peak at what they were eating. And listening. That was the beginning of my intrigue with pasture management. It was an excellent experience for us. They were excellent teachers.

Before the gates to the new age could be opened and their cows let out into nature, Karl especially would have to take the leap of faith that freeing dairy cows from their confinement and the special care and feeding they received there would solve the problem of

Grass has always been the foundation of the prosperity cows brought to Wisconsin.

Ruminants are in the business of converting the plant cell walls of forage crops into energy and protein. That is, cows convert fiber into life. This is why we love them so much. Or perhaps we should really love the microbes in cows' reticulum and rumen that do the digestive heavy lifting.

Forages are the green parts of grass or legumes containing the high quantities of fiber cows live on. (Corn is a grass, in case you forgot.) Farmers, of course, require that cows do more than just live—they need to produce large quantities of milk cheaply. A high-producing cow, for example, consumes as much as forty pounds of forage a day. (Forage is measured as "dry matter.") In addition, she needs to eat nearly twenty pounds of corn or other high-energy grains, plus expensive protein and vitamin and mineral supplements, if she is to do the tremendous work we ask of her. A very high-producing cow requires just over $6.00 a day in feed (about $2,225.00 a year). This represents about one-half of the cost of running a dairy farm, on a per-cow basis. Of this, her forage costs $1.75 a day (about $640.00 a year), about 30 percent of her total feed costs.

So, to the degree that farmers can provide high-quality, digestible forages that

The COW The MOTHER of PROSPERITY

WHi Image ID 8592

their cows relish and turn into milk efficiently, they will profit.

Forages are provisioned to cows as pasture, hay (dried grass), or silage (basically, pickled grass). The quality of forages—and their value as feed—varies significantly from field to field, farm to farm, day to day, and year to year. Provisioning adequate high-quality forages is also highly dependent on the management skills of the farmer.

continued...

Courtesy of the Klessig family

Bill Sixel, Otto Klessig 1912

Otto Klessig (likely the man on the right) is the great-grandfather of the current generation of Klessigs. The hay that he and Mr. Sixel are putting up this summer day so long ago would be—respectfully—rejected by his great-grandchildren today. But it was good enough to create the dairy industry in Wisconsin.

Over the 160 years of commercial dairying in Wisconsin, the quality of forages has made quantum leaps. The hay of bygone days is hardly fit for bedding today, and the hay that fed milking cows fifty years ago is barely fit for nonmilking stock today. The tremendous improvement in the quality and quantity of feeds is the single most important element in the tenfold increase in milk production over the history of dairying in Wisconsin.

New strains of forage crops, better fertilization, more scientific planting techniques, and more and more efficient technologies for cutting and preserving forages have brought huge increases in feed quality and milk quantity. They have kept Wisconsin farmers in business.

spending too much and being paid too little. After all, the incredible historic success of dairying in Wisconsin happened *because* farmers had brought cows closer into their lives. Opening the pasture gates for cows to mostly take care of themselves seemed risky. Could nature—improved nature, to be sure—take over enough of the dairy farmer's chores and costs? Crossing over would also mean that they were willing to consider abandoning the kind of dairying their father and grandfather had done.

The rebels employed their arguments strongly enough to get Karl to agree to a series of experiments. First the heifers, then the dry cows—cows not presently milking—with the heifers (what did they really have to lose?), and finally the rent-paying cows—the milking stock—would begin to fend for themselves on human-improved grazing land.

Here is how Jerry describes the moment when the men opened the gate, literally and figuratively, to enter the new world of farming-by-doing-less:

> We finally had all the fences up, and we pushed the cows out. It was like Karl couldn't open the gate. He just could not open the gate. And finally Robert said, "Get the hell out of the way. I'm going to open that gate, and out they go."

Would their cows thrive on grass as they had thrived with the controlled feeding of the barn? How would they be doctored without the close observation that was the dairy farmer's art? How would they weather rain, black flies, ninety- and fifteen-degree temperatures? Would nature really take care of her own as well as dairy farmers could?

Answers began to come from incidents like this one that Jerry recalls:

> One day when we opened the gate, this one old girl, who wasn't that old, was to the back of the group. I actually got behind her and forced her out the door. Put her in the pasture. She was just all cramped

up, not very limber, and sore. She didn't know what was going on. Almost confused. Two weeks later that same cow was running in front of the group to get out to the pasture. Since then we have an excess of cows because they don't die, they're much healthier.

That's why at the end of winter we say, "It's going to be good here in the next few weeks because Dr. Green [grass] is coming back."

By "releasing" their cows, the men were releasing themselves to develop their own system of successful dairy farming. They would now put together a very different dairy farm, a farm they would *manage* rather than work, a farm they hoped would create a more balanced relationship between themselves and nature. They set to work.

Ten years after they began limited grazing, Heimerl and the Klessigs had converted 750 acres of excellent cropland into managed grazing land, 750 acres that required far less cultivation year after year and much less handling of manure. Less cultivation meant they would not have to invest money they didn't have in expensive equipment. Their old tractors would do. As young Joe Heimerl puts it, he no longer gets to be on a tractor plowing corn land all spring.

While they may have broken from the past, the Saxon farmers were actually *returning* to the past. One hundred years ago cows grazed on the same land they graze on today.

At first, Joe suggests, he had something of an identity crisis when the family converted from human labor to cow labor. For many farmers, plowing and harvesting is deeply satisfying work. Working the land is a fundamental definition of what a dairy farmer does. A well-prepared and well-planted field is a thing of beauty, and a silo full of cow-delighting feed that you put up yourself is deeply satisfying.

But the cost of provisioning cows on pasture is considerably lower than the cost of feeding them harvested forages. And because the Klessigs and Heimerl were keen on reducing costs, they decided to rely as much as possible on feed from their pastures. Because of a number of changes in the way they manage their farm, the amount of milk they got from each cow dropped significantly. But, while production fell, so too did their costs. It has taken the men a while to learn how to get the most of their cows under their new management system. Today, per-cow milk production is on the rise.

However, the men had no intention of giving up a milk check for the five months of winter. They would still need high-quality forage. And if they were to have meaningful milk checks they would also need corn. This was work that had to be done by someone.

"When you can go out to the field and lay on the ground and hear all the munching of all the flowers and sweet alfalfa, the grasses, that munching, that is a cow moment for me. The contentment of them sauntering all around you . . . that's a satisfying moment."
—Elise Heimerl

© Wisconsin Milk Marketing Board, Inc.

So, they turned another page in the farmer-is-self-sufficient textbook of Eddie Klessig and his era. They would contract with someone who did nothing but crop work for hire to plant and harvest for them. (Today they have been able to buy new hay and silage equipment and have returned to harvesting a portion of their forage needs.)

In effect the men were off-loading the traditional physical work of the dairy farmer and freeing themselves to use their minds more. As they allowed the ideal of the traditional dairyman to fade, they began to be much more intellectual farmers. They began to put together an integrated system for caring for their cows at the lowest possible cost based on a return to a grass-based management system.

The key to their plan was to increase the number of cows they milked and could afford to feed. When they began they had a herd of 125; ten years later they had 425. (A general rule of thumb is that it takes about 100 cows to support one dairy farm family in Wisconsin.) So while they still get less milk per cow than more intensive dairies, they have nevertheless greatly increased their cash returns.

The men would not, however, turn their backs on the modern world of dairy farming. While returning to a more natural way of farming was important to them, they mostly saw it as a more profitable way for them to run a farm—and a way to earn enough to support four families on the land they love. They would not become "lost in our own loftiness," as Jerry puts it.

These are dairy farmers, not saints. As Robert says,

> But the object is to still adhere to very high expectations to take care of our environment, take care of our herd, to farm as friendly as we can environmentally, and to make the cows feel as comfortable as they can in their natural environment.
>
> If the cows are happy, it makes us happy. I feel so strongly about that. If we weren't grazing like we do, I doubt very much that I would be dairy farming.

No, not saints, but farmers who wish to enjoy, as best they can in the modern world, the more ancient pleasures of cows. "It is very pleasing," Karl says, "to see cows on pasture."

For the Craves, as for so many other Wisconsin dairy farmers, dairying was and is a family affair—and family business.

The Business of Progressives

࣌

THE CRAVE BROTHERS

George was always looking for a way to do things better;
produce more milk, take good care of our cows, but get a better
price for all the hard work that we put into it. —Debra Crave

EVERY YEAR, DAIRY FARMERS from Japan, China, Europe, and all over the United States travel to Waterloo, Wisconsin, to find out how to care for cows so they will pay in the modern world. They come because the Crave brothers of Waterloo are among the most notable progressive dairy farmers in the country. In 2008 the World Dairy Expo named them Dairymen of the Year.

Brothers Charles, George, Tom, and Mark; George's wife, Debra; and some of their children manage a thousand milking cows, a thousand acres, and dozens of employees. They grow all their own feed on their own land. The manure from their cows provides nearly all the fertility their soils need to sustain their cows. And now it provides enough electricity to light their homes, their cheese factory, and 450 of their neighbors' homes as well.

The Crave families have health insurance. They take vacations. Their children take music lessons, play in youth soccer leagues, and go to college if they want. The brothers exercise their considerable talents and intelligence in work they find rewarding. They provide good livings for their employees. They work together as only a family can. And they have a successful business that will keep growing enough to allow any of their children to continue the family legacy in farming—a legacy of progressivism.

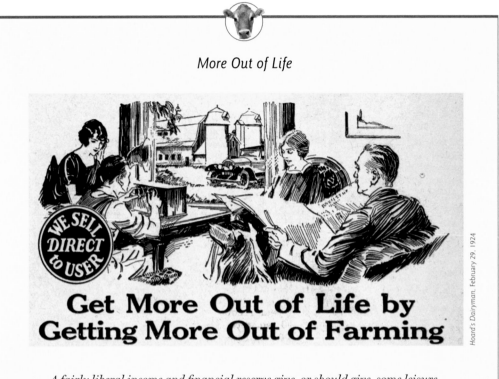

WE SELL DIRECT to USER

Get More Out of Life by Getting More Out of Farming

Hoard's Dairyman, February 29, 1924

A fairly liberal income and financial reserve give, or should give, some leisure. Leisure gives opportunity for study and recreation, without which life becomes one ever-revolving round of work, and results in producing an automatic animal. . . .

This desire to gratify the love for the true and beautiful, which has been growing up by reason of the better education, leads directly to the securing of an income sufficiently large to gratify the more refined and newly acquired tastes.

—Isaac Phillips Roberts, *The Farmstead*, 1900

Dairy farming brought the middle-class life to farmers in Wisconsin. It transformed boot-wearing men into gentlemen who wore shoes in the house. It freed women to tend to the shrine of domesticity where warmth, art, education, self-fulfillment, and family creation were practiced. And it created a place that children wished to stay, or so it was hoped.

Self-development through prosperity—the right to get more out of life: it was the progressives' project realized.

This is a story about how dairy farm management has kept a family on the land and in the company of cows—actually, *returned* them to the land and cows after they had been forced off it by the woes of farming. It's a story of how progressive dairying as practiced by the Crave brothers overcame those woes and allows them to continue doing what they love.

"I grew up," George Crave begins, "on a family farm in Beloit. My dad milked about thirty-five, forty cows. So we learned to feed calves, drive tractors, and harvest crops, working with our father."

When we were younger we just assumed that we'd be farming on our home farm. But when I was a sophomore in high school my dad discontinued farming. At the time he was one of sixty thousand dairy farmers in Wisconsin. And he sold his cows in 1974—low milk prices and just wasn't a very viable business. So he discontinued milking cows.

And so we went and worked for neighbors and were more hired men than anything.

Photo by Mark Henrichs

The Craves today (left to right): George, Tom, Mark, their father, Bob, and Charles. The day this picture was taken, the men were trying to figure out how to repair the main water line into the milking barn. They would do it themselves, because Craves love building and fixing things. Together they built their huge barns. Dairy farming offers endless opportunities to keep busy. For farmers like the Craves, keeping busy is one of the rewards of their business.

It was real depressing for us for quite a while. It was my dream. I just assumed that we were going to just be farming there. And that's the way dad talked, too. But it just didn't work out that way.

The 1970s were difficult years for many farmers in Dairyland, especially those who had gone through the age of intensification during which herds had grown, more land was cultivated, more crops planted and harvested, and more work demanded of the farmer. More and more resources were purchased from off the farm: fertilizer, herbicides, insecticides, and fuel. Bigger tractors and equipment were needed to turn over both the soil and the cash. Many farmers took on too much debt.

And, of course, farmers were victims of their own success. More intense agriculture meant more milk, which meant low prices.

Hands-on small-farm dairying was wearing out farmers. As Tom recalls,

> Back in the '70s [my father] had thirty-five, forty cows. And he was a one-man show. We helped him on the weekends, after school, and things like that. It was frustrating for him to farm that way—and he was a progressive farmer for his time. I remember him saying that the price of milk dropped dramatically. And he had enough. He said, "How can I take care of my family and run a farm when the price of milk goes up and down, and now it just went down dramatically again. It's too hard on me. It's too difficult to make a living this way." Years ago when it was just a single person running the farm, they had to be there all the time.

But Charles, the oldest Crave brother, and George, the second oldest, were determined to be farmers. They were going to take care of cows on their own land. So they bought a farm in the hilly country around Mount Horeb and worked it themselves. George's wife, Debra, describes those years:

> We were married in 1982, and there were some rough years for agriculture at that time. Thankfully I was working in Madison, and we

lived very simply. [The farm in Mount Horeb] was rocky and hilly. I remember George pushing a feed wagon up a hill to feed some heifers.

George is a cow man, and he's just always wanted to milk cows and take good care of them. And so he and his brother did that. They split the duties and raised all their own feed and milked their cows and did a really good job.

It was simpler then . . . we were just happy to milk a small number of cows and do a good job at that. Good production, take good care of the animals, and work with a cooperative to get a good milk price. We would never at that point have thought of making cheese on the farm or building a manure digester or adding more and more cows and more and more brothers. But George is visionary and always had another idea in his back pocket.

Charles, George, and later Tom and Mark decided that if they were to keep together as a dairy family, they would have to grow way beyond the small farming geography of Mount Horeb. They would need flat land and more cows. And they would need a different kind of dairy farming.

So the brothers moved to Waterloo, where they would undergo a phase change in the way of the dairyman: they would—somewhat sadly, perhaps—abandon traditional hands-on dairying for a new, "professional" relationship to their cows and to their land.

As the oldest, Charles has the strongest memories of the intimate relationship with cows that has always defined a dairying life. To this day he is wistful about being among a small group of cows:

Sometimes I wish I had fifty cows and my wife and I could just go out there and take care of those fifty, when you really know every last cow. It might have seemed more intimate. You really knew your cattle a little bit better. Not that we don't know them now. And in fact, we know them perhaps better in a different manner—but it's kind of like, do you want your doctor to know you as a friend or as a professional? So now we know our cattle as a professional.

The cows-are-in-the-barn-and-all-is-right-with-the-world plea-sures enjoyed by dairy farmers still bring comfort and satisfaction to dairymen-managers like the Craves have become. Each of them at one time or another in the day finds his way into one of their large, open freestall barns just to hang out with the cows. A strong dose of cow is a good remedy for a too-strong dose of spreadsheets, broken water pipes, and employees calling in sick.

But for better or worse, the farmer's day-to-day working rela-tionship with cows has been replaced by a day-to-day working relationship with human beings.

The logic of progress and professionalism for farmers like the Craves was unassailable. As George views it in retrospect:

> In 1974 the average cow in Wisconsin produced around 12,000 pounds of milk. My dad's cows probably produced around 13,000 to 14,000 pounds. And now our cows produce 30,000 pounds of milk! You wouldn't have dreamt of this type of production in 1974.
>
> We set goals. At the time it was 18,000 pounds, when we started farming in 1978. And then you shoot for 20,000 . . . that was the magic number, a 20,000-pound-herd average. And that came and went. And [then] you shoot for 25,000, you say, "Well, if we change

"There is a wide range in the quality, capacity and success of merchants, lawyers, doctors, mechanics, and why not in farmers? . . . It is astonishing when you find two farmers living on almost adjoining farms, both patrons of the same creamery, both receiving exactly the same price for their butter, and one farmer receiving 600 per cent more net profit from his cows than the other. . . . It is very evident that something has been at work in all these years to create a great degree of sluggishness in the business intellect of a vast number of farmers who keep cows. . . . The farmer of today has little or no knowledge of the scientific side of his business or of his farm."

—*Hoard's Dairyman*, November 29, 1912

this and change that and keep going, do you dare dream of 30,000 pounds of milk?" And we were able to achieve that.

Everything changes incrementally over the years. You plant a specific type of corn; you plant a specific type of alfalfa; you harvest it at different stages. Science changes. Research changes on the different ingredients that we feed cows. And the housing has changed. And then genetics continually improve. So, just incremental changes over a couple of generations of cows and almost a generation of farmers is incredible.

On their new farm in Waterloo, the Craves set about to improve upon the basic business of cows by being meticulous about every detail of their work. The brothers would not abandon the system of intense farming that had brought them unprecedented gains in milk production and cash flow. But they would become intent on sustaining those gains and the productivity of their land, their cows, and themselves. By being particular about every aspect of dairying, the brothers experienced twenty years of unprecedented progress.

But after those twenty years, the Craves decided that running faster by milking more cows much more efficiently had played out for them. As George puts it:

Looking at really what we've achieved in twenty years, [it's] a very nice farm that we were able to build. But then [we were] saying, what are we going to do for the next twenty years? And really the next twenty years didn't look like they offered us the opportunity to grow at that rate or achieve what we have in the past twenty years.

So what are we going to do? How are we going to grow the family business without just saying we're going to milk more cows and grow more corn and alfalfa?

So good at modern dairying had they become that the family had time, capital, energy, and creativity left to consider new ways to employ their managerial talents and their deep familiarity with the dairy business. And like all dairy farmers, they were deeply frustrated with the chronic low prices for milk and the volatility of commodity

Freestall Barns

For dairy farmers, cow comfort is next to godliness. Getting farmers to think about how cows feel was one of the most important intellectual and emotional shifts on the road to dairy prosperity. *Caring* was both a moral virtue and an economic one.

The science of cow comfort and well-being led to a new kind of dairy barn. Freestall barns have taken the place of iconic tie-stanchion barns, where generations of farmers and cows spent so many cramped hours.

Besides being more comfortable for cows than the barns of old, freestall barns make the work of the farmer easier and far more efficient. Manure drops through slats in the floor and flows into holding ponds (where it can be spread at the optimal time for soil fertility), eliminating much scrapping, shoveling, and carbon-intensive daily trips to the fields. Likewise, feed is efficiently distributed by machines.

In freestall barns cows are always at hand, making it easier for farmers to

Comfortable Cows Give More Milk

Hoard's Dairyman, February 8, 1924

observe them. Cows are easily available for breeding and other ministrations, such as hoof trimming. Freestall barns are easily divided so that cows in various stages of lactation can be separated and treated according to their needs. It is this combination of greater comfort for cows and higher efficiency for humans that has made freestall barns the new icon of the countryside. Someday we may be as nostalgic for the freestall barn as we are for the cramped little red barn of yesteryear.

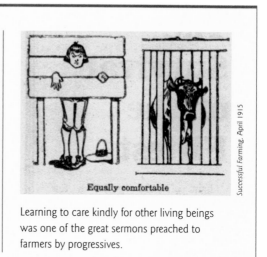

Successful Farming, April 1915

Equally comfortable

Learning to care kindly for other living beings was one of the great sermons preached to farmers by progressives.

markets. One thing dairy farmers didn't seem able to control was the law of supply and demand.

"Unfortunately," George says, "everything progresses, except, it seems, the price of milk."

To add value to what is essentially a commodity, the Craves, like other agricultural producers, began to look around for that "something" for which they could charge more.

At first they considered becoming an organic dairy; at the time, the market for organic milk was growing and supplies were not keeping pace with demand. But the three-year conversion required to become certified organic would, they felt, have put them out of business. As George saw it, for those three years they would still be paid at commodity prices but would have to farm at "1965 production levels because of giving up the technology." Besides, it looked to them as though the rules for organic purity would keep changing, requiring a continuing retrogression to older and older ways of production. As George puts it:

> I believe that [the organic movement] is going to keep demanding more and more of the farmer. I think deep down the organic

movement wants the little red rustic barn tucked into the hillside with a pasture alongside the barn and the husband and wife going out to the barn to milk the cows. And the kids are feeding a couple of calves and heading down to the crick with a cane pole over their shoulder to catch a few bass for evening supper.

Having grown up with the reality of the "little red rustic barn," the Crave brothers decided that the romantic was not for them. As Mark puts it:

> When my kids have a cold or fall off their bike and I take them to the emergency room, the people there who are waiting on us really don't care that I farm. They don't give me a farmer discount. They don't really care if I farm with 1950 or 2007 methods. The cost is going to be the same. So while I could be a martyr and say I'm not going to change because I have higher goals or different goals than that—I guess one of my goals has to be to provide a living.

Certainly, a small herd in a small barn and the idea of exceptional purity are important to some of today's dairy farmers. They have embraced organic dairy farming and the organic lifestyle. For many of these dairypeople, there is a kind of "spiritual purity" that drives them—and their consumers. For some farmers, organic dairying can be quite profitable and a good way of life.

But without making the change to organic, what could the Craves do to increase the value of their milk, their labor, their talents, and their capital? The answer was cheese—just as cheese had been the answer to the first question of dairying, how to make cows pay. Deb Crave had many years of experience in milk marketing, and she and George would take on the cheese business while the remaining brothers divided the other duties according to their interests and skills. The Craves would build a cheese factory a short pipeline's distance from barn to vat. They would return to the very old concept of the farm dairy and convert their own milk into their own cheese using their own expertise and capital. Shipping milk to distant processing factories is a major expense

Progressives and the Agrarian Myth

Richard Hofstadter, the historian of the Progressive Era, argued that progressives set about to free farmers from the "agrarian myth" so they could enter the modern, industrial world and take their place among city dwellers in prosperity and status. As Hofstadter noted in his 1956 book, *The Age of Reform*:

> The United States was born in the country and has moved to the city. . . . What the articulate people who talked and wrote about farmers and farming—the preachers, poets, philosophers, writers, and statesmen—liked about American farming was not, in every respect, what the typical working farmer liked. For the articulate people were drawn irresistibly to the non-commercial, nonpecuniary, self-sufficient aspect of American farm life. . . . [They] admired the yeoman farmer not for his capacity to exploit opportunities and make money but for his honest industry, his independence, his frank spirit of equality, his ability to produce and enjoy a simple abundance. . . . The more farming as a self-sufficient way of life was abandoned for farming as a business, the more merit men found in what was being left behind. . . . The American mind was raised upon a sentimental attachment to rural living and upon a series of notions about rural people and rural life that I have chosen to designate as the agrarian myth. The agrarian myth represents a kind of homage that Americans have paid to the fancied innocence of their origins.[1]

This "fancied innocence" of an idyllic life pure from thought of profits continues to beguile the "articulate people" of today. It also beleaguers dairy farmers who find themselves pressed into a sort of spiritual service in which the wholesomeness of their

continued . . .

Successful Farming, February 1915

THE FARM AS A FACTORY

Today "factory farm" is an epithet hurled at farmers who have too many cows to name. But it was not always so. The metaphor of the farm as factory was employed to introduce the idea that dairy farms should be thought of as integrated systems or, more correct, that they were to be sustainable.

milk and cheese is measured by the purity of their motives. This makes honest discussion between stock raiser and consumer difficult at times.

Dairying is much more complex and interesting than the simple mythical story. The greatness of the progressive movement in dairying—the Wisconsin Idea of Dairying—is that it allows the spiritual and the financial to coexist in a way that benefits both farmer and consumer.

1. Richard Hofstadter, *The Age of Reform: From Bryan to F. D. R.* (New York: Knopf, 1956), 23–24.

for farmers and the environment; a farm dairy eliminates both the cost and the carbon footprint of diesel trucks hauling milk around the countryside.

Looking to escape the treadmill of commodities, the brothers would not produce what large plants could make at lower costs. They would produce what no others could produce: Crave Brothers Farmstead Cheese. They would convert their own milk into cheese no one else had, so it was worth milking cows again.

And they would convert their own milk into a good story. George recounts his first round in the ring against commodity cheese and the American penchant for low prices:

I always tell the story of going to the first [fancy foods] show. We were only open for about six weeks, and we took our cheese in a cup that Deb had designed that tells a little story on the side of the cup: this cheese is produced on our family's cheese factory, where the milk comes from a farm—that we grow our own crops, we produce our own milk, and we farm in harmony with the land. And we go to the food show and introduce ourselves to different people and tell them our little story and show them the cup. And they go, "Oh, that's great. What's your price, what's your distribution, what's your minimum, who's your broker?"

"No, you don't understand, I have this farmstead cheese factory where we farm in harmony with the land, where my brothers produce the crops and they milk the cows and I take the milk and produce a really high-quality, farm-fresh, farmstead cheese, produced right in our own little farm in Waterloo, Wisconsin."

"Oh, congratulations. What's your price, who's your broker, what's your minimums?" I'm, like, "Oh boy, oh boy. This has only so many legs."

Round one went to price and convenience. The brothers adjusted, purity of storyline being a luxury they did not wish to purchase.

Today the Crave Brothers Farmstead Cheese company "buys" about 80 percent of their own farm's milk. With it they make both signature American original cheeses like their own *Les Frères* ("The Brothers") and ethnic specialty cheeses. And because they are a small and highly flexible factory, they also are able to fulfill very particular orders for unusual packages and weights. They also contract with marketers to make private-label cheeses. In other words, the Craves are successful cheese factorymen because they are nimble and willing to do what it takes to satisfy customers.

According to George, their cheese factory has effectively added about two dollars for every hundredweight to the price they get for the milk they sell to themselves, about a 12 percent increase over what their neighbors get. Processing their own milk into their own products has allowed the brothers to hedge against some of the worst volatility in the commodity milk market. Adding greater control to lives is a progressive tenet.

The brothers, like many Wisconsin dairy farmers, take pride in being as

Courtesy of the Crave family

Many dairy farmers have dreamed of transcending the world of commodities and having something no one else has. Today's revival of cheesemaking on the farm is giving some dairymen the chance to do more than just wish their milk well as it leaves their farm in a tanker truck.

independent and self-reliant as possible. For them, sustainability and independence are both good business and their own reward: the yeoman's deeply satisfying reward of standing on his own and relying on what his own farm can produce. The brothers—and other like-minded progressive dairy farmers—are now writing a new chapter in the farm-as-factory book by finding a new way to keep their resources in the virtuous cycle that has historically defined dairying. Today manure not only feeds their soil, it creates electricity for their neighbors.

In 2006 the brothers entered a partnership with a company that specializes in creating electricity from biomass. The company built and paid for an anaerobic manure digester on the brothers' farm. (A second digester was built a few years later.) The Craves' digester uses microorganisms to break down the organic matter in their manure and the whey from their cheese factory into methane gas, which is then burned to produce electricity. This is the methane that would have warmed the globe as it lay on their fields after manure spreading. The company sells the electricity back to the grid, lessening the use of conventionally fired electricity-generation plants. About 450 homes now get their electricity as a result of the Craves' factory farm ethic of parsimony. The electricity alone is valued at $300,000 a year.[1]

While the brothers receive no income from the sale of the electricity generated by the digester, they are now able to store their manure in a way that eliminates the objectionable odors their new, formerly urban neighbors find bothersome; create a more nutrient-available fertilizer for their fields; have excellent free bedding for their cows; and dispose of their whey in an ecologically benign way.

Creating the modern farm-factory is expensive, requiring a sizable concentration of cows to be feasible. However, as with the neighborhood creameries of the past, today's small farmers may be able to pool their manure to be digested in nearby communal digestion plants. This would help solve the small farm's—and small cheese factory's—methane gas problem, which larger operations like the Craves' are now able to do.

Photo by Mark Henrichs

About his father Mark Crave says, "He was a person who always said, there's got to be a better way to do this task or that task. Or we have to be able to make feed better because of this or that. He was a very creative person. So he was always trying to make improvements. And he's pleased that we're able to do that."

Bob Crave is a frequent visitor to his sons' farm, pleased, I should think, that they are prosperous dairymen with much to show for their hard work—hard work he still indulges in with them.

The Craves are successful today because they have been willing to substitute the "simpler" satisfactions of barn, field, and hands-on dairying for the satisfactions of management and the sophisticated and specialized use of their talents as a team. George explains:

> I used to just love cows and I loved milking them and walking amongst them and selecting the matings to produce the next generation of cattle. And I still love that. But it's progressed for me to more of a professional, strategic thinking of, how can we make this farm work this way. We mature as individuals, and you start to focus on different things.

The Crave brothers have spent the past thirty years or so finding a way to stay on the land and among cows to fulfill their father's idea—and the Wisconsin Idea of Dairying—that cows could be made to pay enough for a good life. They have become exceedingly particular in every aspect of the care of cows, soil, markets, and people. And they have been rewarded for being progressives.

One of the first families of Wisconsin cheesemaking: Simon Lepley (born 1863), Cora Emma Lepley (milking), Alice Marie (the baby), Lee Lepley, and Sarah Lepley Burt. According to the family, Lee Lepley, a cheesemaker in Liberty Pole (Vernon County), famously remarked, "I made cheese for forty-five years and made money every year." Alice Marie was purportedly the first licensed woman cheesemaker in the state. And Sarah Burt was the grandmother of perhaps Wisconsin's most decorated cheesemaker of today, Sid Cook, whose father Sam learned his trade from Lee Lepley, marrying along the way one of Sarah's daughters, Merna.

The Ages of Cheddar

ॐ

SAM COOK AND SID COOK

Well, there was nothing [for me] on the farm, and we always
had to get up and milk. You had to get those horses up out of the
field to pasture. Maybe it'd be rainy. And you'd be sopping wet, and
you'd go down in the rain, and the cheesemaker'd step out and
he'd say, "My, what a nice rain we're getting." And I kind of
decided I wanted to make cheese. —Sam Cook

MELBOURNE COOK, "they call me Sam," was born in 1919 in Richland
County, the middle of the Cheddar Belt. Cooks had settled around
Bloom City by the late 1850s. According to Sam, they were people
who, like the other pioneers in Wisconsin, "were just happy with
what they had. Living, you know." The Cooks arrived in Wisconsin
in the era before the cow—or, before the cow became a source of
prosperity for people like the Cooks. Sam said, "If you had a cow you
could raise a family. You had milk to drink, you had butter, you had
cottage cheese, too. You survived, yes."

Sam Cook's career as one of the men who helped transform milk
into money for his neighbors, and himself, encapsulates the great
Age of Cheddar in Wisconsin.

Sam Cook was a "maker"—a man who was paid for each pound
of cheese he made and sold. He worked for his patrons, the farmers who paid him to find a market for their milk by making it into
marketable cheese. His son Sid, on the other hand, is a cheesemaker-
entrepreneur, a man who buys his neighbors' milk from them and

transforms it into cheeses that people do not even know they want, until they taste it.

Sam Cook worked in the period during which Wisconsin cheesemakers learned to master their medium through painstaking improvement in every detail of their craft. Sid works in an era in which Wisconsin cheesemakers are mastering *flavor*.

In 1929, a few years before Sam Cook started cleaning milk cans at his wife's great-uncles' cheese factory, there were 2,499 factories, creameries, and condenseries at country crossroads in the state. These usually were small establishments, supplied by two dozen or so farmers each with a dozen or so cows. On average each employed fewer than three men.[1]

Cheesemakers kept warm while farm boys got wet and cold.

For some boys, like Sam Cook, going to work in the cheese factory meant exchanging a farmer's life for an inside job.

Well, there was nothing [for me] on the farm, and we always had to get up and milk. You had to get those horses up out of the field to pasture. Maybe it'd be rainy. And you'd be sopping wet, and you'd go down in the rain, and the cheesemaker'd step out and he'd say, "My, what a nice rain we're getting." And I kind of decided I wanted to make cheese.

The crossroads cheese factory and creamery were important socially and politically as well as economically for farmers in the early days of associative dairying. Factories often were organized and governed by farmers themselves, serving as training schools for self-governance and community leadership (and sources of disputes, misgovernance, and enmity as well).

In these small-business laboratories, often-parochial farmers were introduced to the desires of people far beyond their own township. Farmers were forced to overcome their let-them-eat-what-we-give-them producer's bias. They began to understand that their livelihoods were linked to people with interests different from their own. These farmer-run businesses set up a dialogue with city people that continues today.

For Wisconsin cheesemakers, marketers, and industry leaders, tuning into the demands of the market was the project that would occupy Sam Cook's era at the vat. The near-fatal collapse of Wisconsin's reputation in the late 1800s as a result of the

"Whoever it was who first seriously took up the business of making cheese for a livelihood, and carried it to a success, and thereby demonstrated to his neighbors, and to the people of the state, that our climate, soil, and the production of suitable food were admirably adapted to the profitable pursuit of the dairy interest, conferred greater and more tangible benefits to the present and future prosperity of the people of the state, than has been done in, almost any other branch of agriculture."

—Hiram Smith, Wisconsin Dairymen's Association president, January 1877

Farmers unload milk at a Wisconsin crossroads cheese factory or creamery, circa 1910. While delivering milk cans every day was a time-consuming chore—one that would later be taken over by contract milk haulers—it afforded often-isolated farmers the chance to hang out with each other. As Sam Cook recounts, "They brought them [milk cans] in with the horses. And you'd see a guy coming down the road, you'd try to get ahead of him. Get in line. Maybe there'd be five or six ahead of you waiting to unload. But you got to talk to your neighbors."

filled-cheese crisis (see page 40) had been the spur toward enforced standards of quality and consistency. Cheesemakers needed to be better trained, equipped with useful technology, and watched with careful eyes. Cheesemaking was moving beyond its this-seems-to-work phase. For the next two generations the more technologically, scientifically, and market-savvy operators would succeed, consolidating their more seat-of-the-pants brethren out of business. This consolidation brought about better cheese and better prices for farmers.

Sam Cook was among those makers who had one foot in the craftsman camp and the other in the science camp. He was granted his state license to "operate a dairy plant 6½ miles northeast of Plain, Wisconsin," in 1947.

Sam and his wife, Merna, bought a run-down factory at Irish Valley and acquired sixteen patrons, through the good graces of a

Six and a half miles northeast of Plain, Wisconsin, half a mile down Irish Valley Road you would have found Sam and Merna's factory and home.

kindly older friend who convinced skeptical local farmers that this upstart from Richland County could make them a few extra cents for their milk. The factory at Irish Valley would be the place where Sid Cook would taste cheese for the first time, the place where the smell of milk wafted into his crib, the place where he fell in love with the cheddar of yesteryear.

In the early days of Sam Cook's operation at Irish Valley, cheese was bought by a buyer who represented companies capable of marketing to city dwellers in the United States and Europe. Sam sold his cheese to a man named Kirkpatrick in Richland Center, who sold it (along with cheese from other local makers), under the name English Gold. Ultimately these cheeses were distributed by big companies like Kraft, Borden, and Armour. "You took what they gave you," Sam says. "We was lucky to sell what we had."

From very early on, the product of small cheese factories was bought up by middlemen, like Kirkpatrick's of Richland Center, who resold it to regional and national distributors and packagers. Often to the dismay of the makers, the local trade in cheese was monopolized by powerful buyers.

By the early twentieth century the large and powerful national marketers catering to the country's newly developing mass market demanded the end of poorly made cheese. *Consistency* was, and remains, the word on the lips of every cheesemaker in the state. Long shelf life, consistent quality, and mild flavors made Wisconsin cheese a huge success in national and international markets. Farmers were enriched and grew prosperous as cheese was drained of its sometimes-eccentric "personality." This was the great achievement of the Age of Cheddar.

No longer would each factory have its own self-propagating culture and molds resident in its walls and aging planks. No longer would any milk that wasn't sour do. Science and the mass market were creating modern Dairyland.

Many small factories went out of business, unable or unwilling to modernize. Many old cheesemakers, born of the craftsmen era, were bewildered and put off by scientific cheesemaking. For example, as Sam explains, pasteurization saved untold millions of pounds of milk and cheese, but "it was an added expense."

> The guys thought, whatever's in [the milk] is going to be in there if it's pasteurized. Ain't going to help anything. If there was a bunch of dirt in there, it's still going to be dirt. Well, they didn't know what they was talking about, really.

Sam Cook is a bridge to the era when modern dairying was being invented. Perhaps he didn't see the world at the beginning, but he made cheese with men who had. And as he made cheese with his son, Sid, he passed on to him some of the "mysteries" of cheese. Sid remembers,

> The first lightbulb went on when I was about three years old. I would go out in the factory and drag a thirty-eight-pound wheel out from underneath the scale and open it up and take my dad's tryer and stick it into the cheese. And [I would] take a sample out and eat it and then push it back in thinking that he wouldn't know that I did it. I think that's really when the lightbulb went on—'cause I liked the cheese. Because I liked the way the cheese tasted. I'm very lucky. I have a tremendous flavor memory. I can remember the cheeses that I tasted when I was a little kid.
>
> We had aged cheddars [stored] that were three, four years old. We would set them back because that's what we liked. We've always made artisanal cheeses in Wisconsin, we just never sold them. We did it for ourselves. Now we're going back to the place we were in 1900.

Sid drove his baby scooter and later his trike around his father's vats. When he opened the door from his mother's kitchen he smelled the warm milk from the plant below. He listened to two generations of old Wisconsin cheesemakers talk cheese and shuffle cards. He watched milk form curds and the cellar's molds perform their magic flavor tricks. And young Sid Cook ate cheese that had been secreted from the mass market, cheeses that *cheesemakers* wanted to eat.

Sid Cook is more than a Wisconsin cheesemaker; he is an artist-entrepreneur whose medium is milk and whose business is flavor. And his business saved a little cheese factory from becoming a small-town relic and quaint reminder of what's been lost.

When Sid finished college (with a degree in political science) he took over his father's Irish Valley factory "because I just didn't know any better." This small roadside factory was strictly a family affair, employing Sid, his father, and his mother, the very epitome of "mom-and-pop" cheesemaking. As Sid and Sam made their cheese, mostly cheddar, they watched as the era of the small local roadside factory was coming to an end.

Once the model of efficiency, these often family-operated places were succumbing to the same forces that had built them in the first place, because now the mass market had become truly massive, with even greater demand for lower prices. During the 1980s and early 1990s small cheese plants were being abandoned as cheddar and mozzarella went looking for ever-greater efficiencies and lower prices.

The old system was breaking down, leaving the small plants to fend for themselves. Sid explains,

> In the old days we sold 100 percent of our cheese to Armour Foods, or we sold it to Borden or Kraft. We don't do that today, because in 1975 Borden stopped buying cheese. They gave us all a month's notice. Fifty plants. "We're no longer buying your cheese after this day." So you had fifty plants that were looking for a cheese market.

Lucky for Sid, a cheese market kept walking into his plant.

> So you know, thirty years ago there were foodies driving around. They weren't called "foodies" then. But they were driving around to small cheese factories. And they'd come in and they'd be asking,

Sam and Merna's Irish Valley factory, circa 1960—a place where the old-timers kept the cheese they wanted for themselves—and the place where young Sid learned about taste.

"You got any real old cheese?" "What's the oldest you got?" "You got anything special that you've set aside?"

There were people that would go to all the different factories because they had a huge interest in cheese and it was their quest to find the best and the most unusual. And, well, if you wanted to sell them some, then you'd sell them some.

So Sid starting selling the cheesemakers' own cheeses, the ones hidden in the cellar, the ones with strong flavor, to these seekers of flavor—just a little at first.

So then the chefs started seeking us out. They would buy cheeses and take them back to their restaurants, cook with them, and then they started ordering them. And people that would come and watch us make cheese would buy cheese.

. . . There's a certain element with cheese that almost is addictive. You can tell when people are sampling. They'll take one. And it will be a little while. Then their hand just goes out. It's just automatic. They can't help it. They don't think about it. Something in their head just

Courtesy of the Cook family at Carr Valley Cheese

Sid on the vehicle he used to scoot around his father's cheese vats. That's Bonnie, Sid's older sister, who now manages one of his Carr Valley cheese stores.

clicks and their hand goes out and they get another piece and they put it in their mouth. . . . That's how you know it's really good.

What we really like to do is get their hand past their hip so they get their wallet out.

Sid was beginning to realize that he could build a business on the art of pleasing people.

The years that Sid had studied flavor in his father's cheese cellar, the years in which milk had seeped into his pores, the years he spent learning the science of milk, and the years making cheddar at Irish Valley gave Sid Cook an almost ancient mastery over his medium.

Well, you know, you open the kitchen door, it's right there. At three or four years old, you open the door, you're going to learn something. I think a lot of it is touch, feel, smell, how the cheese is. Today when I walk into one of the cheese factories, I can tell by how it smells, by looking, by all those things that are right in it. And then I start digging in from there. It's the sort of thing that—it's a natural thing.

Sid Cook knew how to work milk into cheese. Now he was beginning to learn how to work cheese into art. He would save his small-town cheese business by becoming playful with milk, by creating and selling cheeses with some of the complex flavors he found in his own head. Sid would create Sid Cook originals, and he would call them American Originals.

In doing so, he would tap into America's new interest in flavor. During the 1980s Americans were enamored with all things European. After all, Europeans had not forsaken flavor as Americans had in our rush for affordable food for everyone. (Never mind that many Europeans produced their "superior" products in huge, efficient, automated stainless steel industrial cheese facilities.) Some Americans simply had an inferiority complex when it came to the finer things of life. But by the late '80s, California wines were blowing away the cloud of inferiority. We were discovering our own national genius for flavor. Brewers, winemakers, bakers, and cheesemakers began to create flavors never tasted on earth before. The American genius for invention had discovered food. Sid says,

Courtesy of the Cook family at Carr Valley Cheese

> An American Original is a cheese that you just make up. It's not a Gouda that's made in the U.S. It's not a Fontina. It's not an Emmenthaler. It's a cheese that we just make up. It doesn't represent any European [cheese] or any type of cheese from another country. . . .
>
> So, say for example it might be a cow's milk, it might be a sheep milk, it might be a goat milk, it might be a mixed milk. It might be a different kind of blue cheese. . . . It could be a flavored cheese . . . for example, like our Grand Canary, . . . made with sheep, goat, and cow milk,

By the time Sid joined his parents in their factory, the forces of change were already putting pressure on roadside factories like theirs. Sid would guide the family's venerable business into the new age of flavor and financial success.

blended together. It's aged between two and three years and it's marinated in olive oil.

So a cheese that's made like that and handled like that is going to have a completely different flavor profile than any other cheese in the world.

I think it's all about things tasting really good. They can't just be different, they have to be really good.

Sid Cook has won more awards for "cheeses you just make up . . . that are really good" than anyone. Today Sid's Carr Valley Cheese Company, comprising the once nearly defunct little cheese factory

Pizza Triumphant: The End of the Age of Cheddar

It was 1953, and if you were alive you couldn't avoid singing, "When the moon hits your eye like a big pizza pie, that's amore" along with Dean Martin. Perhaps you knew something about pizza but had never actually seen one. Pizza was still ethnic food and mozzarella an almost imperceptible portion of U.S. cheese sales. Indeed, according to the USDA Agricultural Statistical Service, production of all Italian cheeses was around one-tenth that of cheddar alone in 1955. By 2003 mozzarella had surpassed cheddar as America's favorite cheese. And by 2007 mozzarella represented more than one-third of all cheese produced in the United States. Today the house of Wisconsin cheese is built upon a firm foundation of pizza. So, "when the moon hits your eye like a big pizza pie," that's really good for Wisconsin.

in tiny La Valle, Wisconsin, and sister plants in Fennimore and Mauston, has sales in the many millions of dollars and employs eighty people. Sid Cook also "employs" hundreds of cows scattered on thirty small family-operated farms to which he pays top dollar for their milk. And he is the largest buyer of goat and sheep milk in the state.

While about 20 percent of his sales come from his own seven Carr Valley stores, Sid's cheeses are also distributed by sixty dealers selling to fancy food stores and natural foods emporiums.

While Sid is justly proud of his American Originals, he seems to take particular delight in what he sees as a new Golden Age of Cheddar. One of his most popular cheeses, his bandage-wrapped, cave-aged cheddar, is a reverential reconstruction of the flavor of the old-timers, a sort of homage to the cheddar of history. "Things are coming around full circle," Sid says.

> We're going back to wheels again because we've discovered that there's a huge difference in the flavor profile. There's a huge difference in the way it tastes and the way it's perceived.

For example, the cave-aged wheels are [in] a cooler over there that represents a cellar environment of 53 degrees, 85 percent humidity. When my grandfather or great-great-uncle put cheeses in the cellar, it would be very, very similar to that. The molds would be coming off what was native in the plant; that's what's going to grow on that bandage. They would use cream or make butter and rub the rinds or use lard [to keep] the moisture in. But it was fine that they molded. And those molds that grew on the outside are going to feed off the proteins. There are going to be enzymes produced. The flavors of the cheeses are going to be earthy. The way the cheeses taste is going to be very individual. That's what we're doing now.

When my [great-] great-uncle Ed Lepley started making cheese, it was 1883 and he was fourteen years old. And it's probably not a whole lot different than the environment, as far as curing, that we're doing today. So here again, the place that we're going back to is the place that we came from in 1900.

© Wisconsin Milk Marketing Board, Inc.

The deeper art of making cheese according to Sid: "It's more than technical. It's a completely different side to the business—it's like, yes, I have the technical side with the book learning and the scientific side and all the classes. But the other side of it just is natural. You just know when it's right and when it's not."

American cheese lovers should be grateful that Sam Cook decided to take an inside job in the cheese factory so many years ago.

Behind the renovated barn that the Daniels family calls home are paths that have led cows from barn to fields of green for one hundred years or more. On a mild summer day, Laura's Jersey cows are off to work—if you can call it work—in the pastures.

The Cow-Driven Life

⌇

LAURA DANIELS

*Dairy farming really isn't about putting milk into the
bulk tank and the truck comes and takes it away and you get
your paycheck. It's really that you are 100 percent responsible
for the well-being of hundreds of animals. Every day!
They need you. They really do.* —Laura Daniels

To VISIT LAURA DANIELS at her Heartwood Farm, head north off
Highway 18 just outside of Cobb in Iowa County. If you pass the
wind turbines, you've gone too far. Now you will be driving down
one of those valley roads that leads you into a kind of time warp,
depositing you in a place where things move at the self-satisfied pace
of bovine contentment. It is a slow coun-
try dance in which cows lead and humans
keep up. And there is much keeping up to
do to care well for cows.

Laura Daniels is a smile in overalls and
a Dutch boy haircut. Her joy is the result
of her cow-driven life, a life that has led
her to a herd of her own and to a relationship with 280 Jersey cows.

Cows have brought Laura the life she
really wanted to live, a life in the country
caring for animals and encouraging green
stuff to grow. It took her a while to get
here, though.

Caring for cows brings a smile to Laura Daniels's face.
Except, of course, when the temperature is below zero
and the price of milk below sixteen dollars.

ONE WOMAN'S SUCCESS

By MRS. J. H. McROSTIE

Successful Farming, April 1913

Laura learned about cows and how to care for them on her parents' dairy in Burlington in Kenosha County. There her step-father, Bob, introduced her to the mutual benefit society formed by humans and cows. As with many relationships, especially those begun in childhood, Laura's relationship with cows started with the simple and happy experience of just being together with Frisky, her first show calf. As she describes those early experiences:

> For us showing cows was about really spending time with them. That was what I did all summer—train these calves and paint their toenails and give them a bath every day. So you just spend so much time and you get so used to being near them. Once they're comfort-able and not afraid anymore, they'll just be there. They'll just be beside you. It's really an incredible thing. But they're so gentle. And they really are just so easy to be with.
>
> I think that any relationship, whether it be [with] the cows or my employees, it really has to be reciprocal. It has to be a two-way street. If it's not, it doesn't work. It's just as true with cows as it is with people. It really is. So I just think that you have to nurture that. You have to let that grow.

The relationship between a dairy farmer and his or her cows grows from an early companionship. This is the time when the important lessons in caring are learned. This caring is the soul of dairying and, for many, its deepest reward. And it is these early lessons in caring for calves that prepare future dairymen and -women for their responsibility for the care and comfort of cows. Dairy farm families know this very well indeed, for they consciously teach the lessons of caring. In a way, calf cuteness is the basis of the dairy industry.

In its basic formulation the relationship between cows and farmers is simple: we feed and house them, and they provide us a milk check. But for those with a cow-driven life, it is a much more interesting, complex, and happy affair.

Laura Daniels's companionable relationship with calves and her companionable relationship with her stepfather in his barn launched her young mind on all sorts of "how come" questions about cows.

How come this cow is so beautiful? How come this cow eats so well? How come this cow gives Bob more milk than this other one?

How patient Bob was after the first hundred questions is a matter better left to family history. However, we do know that he was an encouraging teacher and a man who believed Laura would learn best by doing. While only in eighth grade, Laura pipsqueaked up: "Bob, I think we could use this other bull. You never buy any semen from this other company, and they have this really good bull."

"Fine," he said, "you be in charge of it."

So even before she was in high school, Laura was in charge of the improvement of the family herd. She had begun the intellectual portion of her dairy career as she pored over bull catalogs and monthly production reports to select the best sires for her family's cows, in order, she says, "to make good cows better."

Laura, her mother, and Frisky in 1986. The proud smile indicates the budding of a cow-driven life.

Courtesy of the Daniels family

From very early on the dairy clergy knew that the obligation to care for cows was taken on at a young age.

Hoard's Dairyman, August 23, 1912

BEGINNERS IN DAIRYING

Like many young people with a calf-driven life, Laura also took up one of the important arts of the dairy farmer: the art of improving the beauty and usefulness of dairy cows.

Besides her interest in the art of the cow, Laura was also interested in art for its own sake. She recalls:

> I always had a bipolar thing happening through high school. I was very artistic, and I really loved to paint. The art room was my study hall and my afterschool class. I was always there. I just loved all of it. I just loved creativity. And I knew that I loved dairy cows.

Laura and her mother visited the Milwaukee Institute of Art and Design to see if painting would be a happy alternative to dairy farming, a place where Laura's great well of creativity could find its best expression—and provide her a good living. Or, could she find a way to be creative and still be involved with cows? For many young people like Laura, the world where things grow and cows low is

"I liked your talk about sentiment in dairy work. You said that to succeed one must be in love with the cow. I wanted to get up then and tell the audience that there was at least one young dairyman on the road to success. Just before the morning session of the convention I saw a boy, just a chubby, little fellow of ten or twelve years standing by the head of a little Jersey heifer. . . . The little fellow placed one arm around the heifer's neck, placed his mouth to her ear as if to whisper to her and then pressed his lips to the eye of the little beauty. I imagine he said to her, 'Do your best, Jersey love, get a blue ribbon if you can, but if you get none I will love you just as well as ever.' . . . This boy will surely be a successful dairyman."

—Letter to the Editor, *Hoard's Dairyman*, March 23, 1912

important to them. They love agriculture even if they don't quite want to milk every day.

Laura enrolled in the University of Wisconsin at Madison in dairy science and agricultural journalism. She would study both cows and the creative art of talking about them.

As it has for so many dairy farmers, the university played a huge role in the development of Laura's ability to think through the hugely complex business of caring for cows and getting them to take care of farmers. As she puts it, "Really, really, at the base of it, they were teaching you how to think." This thinking about how to care for cows is one of the central tenets of the Wisconsin Idea of Dairying.

Cows were still important and interesting to Laura. But would they play a central role in her life again? Could she make her home without them?

My summers during college were sort of spent figuring things out, like where I was going to go and what would be a good path for me. My first summer I went home and worked on my family farm. I have two brothers who were set to take over the farm. And they could have made room for a third, but I don't think our personalities would be a good match. This was the point where I realized I was never going to come back to that farm. It wasn't going to work.

After she graduated, Laura took a job as an itinerant dairy nutritionist visiting hundreds of farms and working with farmers and their cows. These farms are where Laura would study the practical arts of good husbandry and learn that there were many ways to exercise her talents on the farm.

Mostly [farm visits] got me in close contact and helped me build really good, strong relationships with really great farmers—people who are inspirational and who truly love what they do, and are good at it, and who appreciate being outside and being with the cattle. And who have the entrepreneurial spirit.

I ended up working in nutrition for about nine years. It was like a training course the entire time for being a farmer myself. That was an important time [because] I realized that I could do it myself.

But things had to fall in place before that could happen. So it was like you tuck that knowledge away and forge ahead. I had a great job. I had a good income. I was working with all these incredible people. And I bought my first house. And I started to really build equity.

"No interest can be more vital to the farmer himself, than that his sons and daughters should be interested in the vocation in which he is engaged."

—I. J. Clapp of Kenosha, addressing the Wisconsin Dairymen's Association, January 1879

As a result of her studies with "people who are inspirational and who truly love what they do," Laura must have realized that dairy farming could offer her much more than a paint-by-numbers project. Instead she could paint the life she wanted, a life that would include her beloved cows and her creative project for their improvement. She realized she could become a farmer-entrepreneur-artist and create a profitable herd and a good life through her own creative intelligence.

Photo by Mark Henrichs

The relationship between farmer and cow is complex, like all good relationships. Laura's daughter Julia is working on that relationship in this picture.

Then she met Jarred Searls, a man "who really thought I could set the world on fire, who thinks I can do pretty much anything." Jarred, who works off the farm as a beef cattle nutritionist, would be Laura's cheerleader and adviser more than her dairy helpmate. Together they would work to create that herd, and family, of their own.

In early conversations that Jarred and I had, I'm like, "So, you know I've always been kind of thinking about having a dairy farm." And he'd say, "Well, sure. Yeah!" And he truly believes, if you think things through and make good decisions and treat your employees well, you can be a success.

One night we were going to dinner with some friends, and they were late. So we had like half an hour. And I said, let's get out the notebook. And we started writing down: a cow will cost $2,000; each stall costs about $1,500. . . . So we started to figure out how much money to borrow. Which made me think about how much money we had to have. How much equity we needed to have. It was very much where we were thinking it through, like *really* thinking it through.

So that was when I realized, oh, it's going to happen. It's going to happen. It's going to happen.

One of the most important things Laura and Jarred had to think through was how they could have a herd of cows without being tied down by the labor demands that dairy families on traditional farms, like the one Laura grew up on, are subjected to. Laura and Jarred wanted their weekends off, time for their children, and freedom from the tasks they weren't suited for. (I'm not supposed to tell you this: Laura told me that Jarred isn't very good with machines but that he is getting better at it.)

Fifty cows in a conventional tie-stall barn, milked seven days a week by the farmer and her husband, was not the picture Laura wanted to paint. If she and Jarred were going to do this huge thing, they were going to have enough cows so they could afford to hire employees and be profitable enough so they could contract with others to farm their land for them. Laura was going to specialize in the thing she does best: she would care very well for her cows so they would take care of her and her family.

My husband says that every company has the thing that they do best. Right? Well, we make the milk. So we don't do the field work. We really focus on taking good care of our cows. And really making the milk.

Next Laura and Jarred would have to find a farm, a place that would support enough cows and a place where they wanted to spend the rest of their lives—a place they loved and could create for themselves. Laura says,

> I sort of believe we all end up where we're supposed to be. I really believe that my family was supposed to end up at this farm. When we came to this farm and we looked it over the first time, it just sang to us. We just knew this is where we should be. We've just trusted that.

But they also needed to trust their numbers. Could this farm, in this place, with these cows, this kind of barn, this number of tillable acres, this amount of pasture support enough cows to let Laura and Jarred live the lives they wanted? Could they convince both themselves and a banker that they could make cows pay?

> It'll be interesting maybe ten years from now when I can sit down with the banker and say, "Why did you really do that? We know you didn't have to. A lot of other guys didn't. What was it about us that you believed in?" What I think right now is that it wasn't so much about the farm background. Although that was necessary, that wasn't what did it.
>
> It was really about drive. It was about work ethic. And it was about, "Are they going to stay up all night if that's what it takes? Are they going to sell everything but their children if that's what it takes?" They had to really believe in that: those core values. Deep down, are these the kind of people who are going to get it done? 'Cause that's what it takes to be a farmer. Truly.

It is funny how fulfilling our destiny sometimes begins in the most matter-of-fact way. Laura and Jarred signed the papers to buy their farm at midday; that evening Laura was milking *her own* herd. Now she had 240 creatures dependent on her and her alone for their

Buying the Farm

If you want to be a dairy farmer with a farm of your own, what will it cost?

First, cows. You'll need a minimum of seventy-five cows to make a go of it, so that's what you will buy. On average, good commercial cows might cost $2,375 each. Seventy-five will cost you $178,125 to fill your barn.

Because you want to be a complete farmer, you will need a full complement of equipment: a good-size tractor, planting and hay-making equipment, corn-harvesting machines, a feed mixer, a front-end loader, milk line and stainless steel milking equipment, and more. For the average seventy-five-cow dairy, equipment requires an investment of $153,650.

You'll also need a farm with enough land to provide for the feed needs of seventy-five cows, a barn, heifer sheds, maybe a milking parlor, a silo or two, and a house to live in. You might rent some of the land you'll need, but let's say you buy all the land and buildings. You'll need $410,250.

Together with your banker (if you can find one), you will need $742,025 to become a dairy farmer.

well-being. Imagine what it was like for her to stand among *her* cows for the first time. It was, she says, "a whole lot different when you're writing the checks."

Laura had become a dairy farmer.

With one turning of the clock she had also become the steward of 160 acres of hilly land. (She also rents nearly 400 additional acres.) She became responsible to the soil, to keep it fertile and in place for the next one hundred years so it will continue to support cows and families. And she had become responsible to everyone in Wisconsin for keeping her streams clean—a responsibility she and Jarred take so seriously that in 2007 they received the Conservation Farmer of the Year award from their local Trout Unlimited chapter.

She had also become an employer, responsible for creating a genuine cow-caring organization. Laura would become a teacher to her five full-time and four part-time employees, imparting the lessons she had learned—especially those she had been taught by cows.

There are many things to think about—or worry about—when you are in charge of your own dairy farm: whether it will rain on your new-mown hay, whether your employees care enough about your cows, what will happen to the price of milk and your debt to the bank, and how you will get everything done.

Early on the most important thing that I learned from cows is patience. You have to be so very patient. And I'm not very patient by nature. I really like to make things happen fast. But with animals that doesn't work. You learn early that you have to be gentle and you really have to be patient. So the way that I've come along in working with cows is always to wait for the cue from them, to sort of listen in

The Hired Man

One of the distinctive propositions on a dairy farm is the question of help. These dairy queens must be fed and brushed and milked and Governor Hoard and Mrs. Howie have really made us believe must be petted and caressed. It requires good, careful men to develop and handle them with profit, and such men are not always easy to find.

—Mrs. J. Q. Emery, addressing the Wisconsin Dairymen's Association, January 1906

The hired man on Wisconsin dairy farms is the stuff of literature and legend. But he was also a necessity, for without landless men it is unlikely there would have been a Dairyland at all. The same is true today.

During the age of wheat, employment was seasonal for men without the means or proper birth order to own land. Without steady employment—and the wives that permitted—many restless and landless young men abandoned Wisconsin for the gold rush, for free lands farther west, or for growing cities. The resulting lack of laborers for harvests and farm chores

WHi Image ID 4770

Finding reliable people to do the milking has been one of the great challenges of dairying in Wisconsin. These hired men are milking at a certified dairy sometime around the turn of the previous century. Today many milkers are Hispanic immigrants.

was a chronic difficulty for farmers and Wisconsin's rural economy.

But the dairy cow and her demands for attention helped create a stable labor market, especially after the invention of winter milking made possible by the silo. Younger sons of farmers and new immigrants were put to work on neighbors' farms, allowing them to accumulate the capital and experience they needed to begin their own farms. Many of today's great Wisconsin family dairy farms were started by men who learned dairying as hired men. And certainly many of these families were created when a hired man and a farmer's daughter married.

Dairying has always been a labor-intensive business requiring outside help, especially as farmers have smaller families and as their children abandon the country, leaving their parents with too much work to do to thrive. While the age of intensification replaced muscles with machines, it brought with it the necessity to milk more cows and cultivate more land. Today cows are milked three or even four times a day. Hired milkers are replacing family labor as they have always done.

According to the National Agriculture Statistics Service of the U.S. Department of Agriculture, one-third of all hired dairy farm workers in Wisconsin speak Spanish as their primary language.[1] On many of our larger farms there would be no milk without these immigrants from the south. And,

Photo by Mark Henrichs

Laura's milkers, Marisol Ramirez and Alejandro Garcia. Good milkers must speak quietly to cows if the cows are to let down their milk.

as with past immigrants, these workers are changing the social landscape of Dairyland and keeping it "in milk." Perhaps today's hired laborers, like many immigrant hired men of the past, will go on to own dairy farms of their own.

1. USDA/National Agricultural Statistics Service, "2007 Dairy Producer Survey" (July 2007), www .nass.usda.gov/Statistics_by_State/Wisconsin/ Publications/Dairy/dairyproducer2007.pdf, 3.

the way you can listen to animals. And wait and respond with what they need.

I think that that has carried through in such a huge way in how I manage my dairy today. And I try hard to teach all the people that I work with here that they need to learn that lesson first, too.

The first thing, more important than any other thing on our entire farm, is to be gentle with our cows. The cows are the most important things here. They are the reason we're here. They're the reason we're in business. And Jarred and I have so much money invested in these animals that they're the ones who make the money back for us. We have to care for them as gently as possible. So we have rules about how high your voice should be. Whether or not you should whistle. We're always doing training on how we can be more gentle with our cows. So, that's number one. More important than anything else, I tell them, "You remember to be gentle with my cows."

Laura spends as much time as possible among her cows with her expert eye peeled. She milks every morning because she finds it soothing and because milking keeps her in touch, literally, with her cows.

She watches her cows as they eat and poop. She watches them as they walk to see if they are well. She shades her eyes so she can watch them in the pasture while they graze and ruminate. She watches their sex lives and their pregnancies. She especially watches their calves.

And she spends lots of time with her employees, "just listening" and watching them care for her cows, her land, and her water. She is writing the checks, after all.

Laura became a businesswoman, but a businesswoman seeking the more soul-satisfying pleasures of her ancient profession. As she describes it:

Farming is hard work. The days are long. And the work is hard. And if you don't stop and really appreciate all the little things that are developing around you, it can really become cumbersome. Right now the sky is just so blue and the clouds are just puffed white. And

Laura and her hired man and experienced adviser Dave Foley in the conference room at Laura's farm. These professional discussions and planning sessions are important, for it is here that ideas and reality meet. Dave retired from his own nearby farm a few years ago. Because Laura comes from flatland farming country, Dave's experience in farming these rolling hills is vital to her operation.

the sunrise and sunset. Oh, I wish I had a camera, 'cause the cows will be grazing on the hillside and the sunset is behind them. And when you clip a pasture and the grass comes back nice and green and you know you get to graze it again in six days. All those little things. You step back from the hard work and say, "That's why we're here. That's why we're doing this."

Selecting Men for the Barn

Over time, those willing to care for cows were "selected" to remain dairy farmers.

While farmers were selecting the best cows for their barns, the dairy cow was beginning to "select" the people who would care for her. Cows are not for everyone. They require an emotional skill set that sets a premium on patience, routine, quiet, and caring attention to another being's happiness.

Developing the virtues of a dairy-man required, as the agricultural press insisted, that the men who would care for cows needed to be "gentle-men." "Speak to a cow as you would a lady" was a popular admonition in the early days of dairying. The need to transform sometimes rough-hewn and gruff pioneer farmers into patient, kindly, and considerate gentlemen was one of the most common sermons of the agricultural preachers of the time. The making of gentlemen was, like all things progressive, seen as good for both business and the betterment of families and human-kind as a whole.

The real transformation of farmers into dairy gentlemen happened through selection. They were, you might say, selected for their fitness for caring for animals. As time went on, fewer and fewer men were forced by birth, lack of education, or want of opportunity to stay on the farm. Those who chose to stay and care for cows were those who found that being a rustic gentleman fit their personalities and values. Those who enjoyed quiet and wordless interaction found a home in the barn. Those for whom the simple demands of the cow matched their own modest needs found comfort and happiness among cows. And those willing to care found profits. So, the cow has selected us.

Laura takes great pains to explain that dairy farming, like other great professions, is about earning a good living *only in a certain way*, a way that can bear scrutiny from reasonable people:

You can really trust us. Farmers are doing a good job. We're doing a good job taking care of our animals. We're doing a good job taking care of the land. We're doing a good job keeping the water that runs off of our farms clean. We care about those things. This isn't a machine where all we care about is producing milk and income. It's just not like that.

People who need that are not drawn to farming. People who need involvement with the earth and need to be near animals and need to be outside and sort of need to have their own space, those are the people who are farmers.

Mike Gingrich (left) and Dan Patenaude enjoying life with their cows in the pasture

Forward to Yesterday

꒜

DAN PATENAUDE AND MIKE GINGRICH

We had always thought a cheese business on the side might be attractive, because we had heard from old cheesemakers that the best milk for making cheese was always that spring milk—or [it] used to be, when cows always went outside in the springtime and grazed through the summer. . . . We thought we were producing milk with special flavor properties because of the grazing and had no way to really take advantage of that, without developing a product to sell direct to the market. —Mike Gingrich

DAN PATENAUDE IS A PROGRESSIVE CONSERVATIVE. By that I mean he's really interested in finding new ways for people to live by the old ways. Mike Gingrich is an engineer. By that I mean he's really interested in doing things right. Both are dairymen—which means they're deeply interested in making their living among cows.

They are also partners in one of the most renowned dairies in the country, a dairy they built out of nothing but their own desires to live on the land.

Dan's and Mike's story—and their wives' as well—is about how they took the raw materials of Dairyland and created a satisfying, productive, and profitable way of life for themselves. Along the way they have become avatars of a new, old way to be dairy farmers in Wisconsin.

Let's begin with Dan, a native of the dairy country of Calumet County. Like all true conservatives, Dan believes that nature has the essentials figured out pretty well. And as a conservative he worries that these ancient arrangements are threatened by humans' predilection to squeeze too much out of nature, to the detriment of both nature and humankind. Dan's worries started him on his path to finding a way to farm without having to squeeze nature too hard.

In the early 1970s Dan was a "Whole-Earther," a man imbued with the progressive and optimistic spirit of those heady times when many people thought it possible to balance the needs of nature and humans. Humans would be stewards, not lords, of nature, and nature in turn would provide nicely for humans' economic needs, as long as they were modest. It would be a good way to live.

After he graduated with a degree in conservation from the University of Wisconsin–Stevens Point, Dan searched for a good life and a living outside the modern world beginning in the late 1970s with wife Jeanne on a small farm near Spring Green. Dan says:

> [The] time came for us to make a decision about where we were going to live. We just thought it'd be interesting to live out in the country. We didn't know what we were going to do there. We found a place we liked, [with a] nice little trout stream running through it, and jumped in.
>
> We had a neighbor across the road from us who milked about a dozen cows. A single woman. Her cousin was the hired man. She was born and raised there as her father [had been], and her grandfather was the original homesteader on the farm we were on across the road. So for lack of something more productive to do, I started helping her out. One thing led to another. We bought her cows in 1980 and started milking out there. I only started farming to avoid having to have a real job.

While Dan began farming to avoid having a real job, Mike Gingrich had a career. As an engineer with the Xerox Corporation in Southern California, Mike was already advancing up the corporate ladder. Mike, his wife, Carol, and their young family had to move often; it was an unsettled, suburban way of life. Mike and Carol were interested in putting down deeper roots. As he explains,

> My mother's family were all dairy farmers in Michigan. And when I was small I spent every summer on that farm. The more I worked for a big company, the less I liked it and the more I thought that farming would be a much more attractive lifestyle, that my children would love it as much as I did.
>
> So we bought a small dairy and about thirty cows [outside Spring Green]. We had a stanchion barn setup just like our neighbors and grew alfalfa and corn in the fields. We fed the cows stored feeds, and milked year-round, and calved every month of the year. So it was 365 days a year, twice-a-day milking. Really tied us down some.
>
> And the economics were pretty dismal. Carol became the nurse for the local school system. Had it not been for her salary, we could not have lasted for as long as we did. Some years, we barely broke even.
>
> We actually sold that farm in 1986, and I went back to work for Xerox for a few years. Our oldest children were in college, so we had college tuition bills to pay. But we moved back here after we got those financial obligations squared away.

While Mike took a hiatus from his dream, his friend Dan—they had been neighbors and had developed a friendship—was working on cutting the Gordian knot that binds dairy farmers to too much toil for too little profit. Dan was learning that it might be possible to deconstruct the ever-intensifying system of modern agriculture by moving forward to a new and improved *past*. Perhaps nature could yield a satisfactory living without his having to squeeze too hard. Dan had begun to believe that profitability for small farmers lay in drastically cutting costs by getting nature and cows to do much more of the work—work they did naturally, on grass.

> What happened was that it didn't get any more expensive for the cow to walk around and feed herself and spread her manure, but [she] can still walk around at the same price she did fifty years ago.

I started to figure out how to produce milk cheaply, and the cheapest time to do that is in the summer. When you think about it, the feed only grows in the summer, and these animals need forages. And if you look at wild ruminants, they have a cycle where they have a flush of feed, they breed and reproduce on that flush of feed, and when the feed goes down for the season, they go down for the season. So nature operates on this principle.

While Dan was experimenting with his conservative let-nature-do-more-of-the-work idea, Mike and Carol had only deferred their dream to make a living among cows. Mike says,

We came back and saw Dan and Jeanne every summer and kept talking to Dan about the rotational grazing he had started in the early '80s. He was getting some experience with it and telling me about it. And I was interested in it, because I felt like it was a much better lifestyle-type of dairy farming that does not involve much machinery. I never really was too fond of machinery. And the more I looked at it and talked to Dan about it, it seemed like grazing was preferable to the type of dairy farming I had been doing. And we decided, collectively, that that was a good way to produce milk, but it had to be done on a larger scale than Dan was doing it or I had [done it]. We bought this farm [in Dodgeville] in 1994, together, and got a herd of 150 heifers that first year, whereas Dan's herd was about 30 and my herd had been about 30. So it was a much bigger operation. And it looked like we had significant cost advantages at this scale and with this management scheme. And it has worked out well. In fact, once we got it up and running, we felt that it did not take both of us to keep it going. So, we kind of sat back a little bit and thought, well, what could we do with this enterprise?

We had always thought a cheese business on the side might be attractive, because we had heard from old cheesemakers that the best milk for making cheese was always that spring milk, or [it] used to be when cows always went outside in the springtime and grazed through the summer. When they first got on that fresh grass

New Pastures Aplenty

© Wisconsin Milk Marketing Board, Inc.

Good pastures have always been promoted as the foundation of dairying in Wisconsin—for it is these fields that grow themselves that feed our cows, who feed us.

The thrilling moment in the life of a cow is that wonderful day in late May when, after a long winter of confinement in the barn, she is again "turned out" to the pasture. That gala day stirs up all her old instincts and hereditary memories. Playfulness except in the calf is rare among cattle, but in the first hours at pasture the whole herd will often indulge in a wild rush, circling the field with tails carried erect, high over the back like banners and with strange awkward cavorting and galloping—for all the world like the rush of a lot of youngsters let out of school. . . . The real romance for the cow as well as her owner lies in those first golden weeks of early summer. —Jared Van Wagenen, *The Cow*, 1922

Our dairy cows began their commercial lives foraging for themselves, first on wild grasses and then on improved grasses sown to provide them with feed they could milk on. It was a neat arrangement in which cows fed themselves on grasses that pretty much grew themselves. With the invention

continued . . .

of winter milking and the great thrust forward to make cows really pay, dairy farmers realized they would need to carry succulence to their cows, and in greater quantity and quality than the pasture could provide.

While turning cows out to pasture never disappeared in Wisconsin, it faded as a financially significant source of consistent nutrition. Cows simply produced prodigious amounts of milk when they could eat consistently high-quality forages and supplements in a mixed ration, all day and all year long. Keeping cows close to home made it possible to give them more than they could get by themselves. It was a costly arrangement but one that paid off well.

Today many Wisconsin dairy farmers are rethinking the costs and benefits of intensive feeding. In the early 1990s, a new tame grass movement emerged and began to catch the imaginations of farmers who desperately wanted to know if there was an easier and less expensive way to make a living on the land.

This movement is called rotational grazing or intensive management grazing and is different from the old system of continuous grazing, whereby cows went through fresh grass with no thought for tomorrow.

Proponents of the movement are called "graziers." They give great thought to tomorrow by managing a system of pastures in such a way as to give their cows fresh, delightful grass every day from May through October. In these systems, cows provisioning themselves can satisfy 30 percent or more of their yearly feed requirements. The cost of pasture-provided forage is said to be about one-half the cost of the same quality feed brought to the cows.

Dan Truttmann, a dairy farmer outside New Glarus, moves his simple electric fence to open a new paddock for his grazing cows. Unlike haying with heavy equipment, this is a job that his children can join him in. For modern farm families, this is another good reason to be graziers.

Most graziers divide their scientifically improved pastureland into a number of paddocks, each sized to feed the herd for a day or two only, depending on rainfall. By moving a simple, portable fence, the farmer moves the cows onto new grass before they have eaten the plants too low for regrowth. As a paddock regrows during the season, cows are allowed back onto it. Moving the cows to new paddocks takes little time and effort. Likewise, once pastures are first seeded there is little a farmer must do to maintain them year to year. These farmers neither reap nor do they sow (at least for eight to ten years). Of course, because winter has not been revoked in Wisconsin, graziers must also provision their cows with hay, silage, and corn. Nearly all rotational graziers feed stored feeds as well, even during the summer.

In all, managed grazing seems to offer a less intensive and, to its advocates, easier way to farm.

the flavors in the milk just came through in the cheese and made a wonderful-tasting cheese. So we thought, well, rotational grazing is really giving them spring pasture for a good part of the year. You are managing those pastures so that the cows get new grass every day.

We thought we were producing milk with special flavor properties because of the grazing and had no way to really take advantage of that, without developing a product to sell direct to the market.

And every book I read about European cheeses raved about the pastures and how wonderful the cheeses are at a certain time of year because the pastures are new.

Mike believed there was splendor in their grass—and possible financial value as well. So he set out to package that splendor in a way that kept it intact from pasture to table. Mike believed—rightly, it turned out—that he could return cheesemaking to its cottage-industry roots and reverse, in a small way, the flow of milk into the large industrial system and mass market that had defined dairy production for the previous 120 years.

So rather than waving good-bye to their milk at their farm gate and watching it go off to be mixed with the milk of hundreds of other farms to produce an acceptable "average" product for an "average" milk price, Mike Gingrich and Dan Patenaude would package their own milk into their own cheese.

At this point, in the late 1990s, the idea of making cheese exclusively from grass-fed cows seemed to most in the industry like a return to an outdated form of production. There was little sense that a market even existed for something that had died out sixty years before. Who would care what the cows ate?

No one, Mike must have felt, could possibly care as much as he would to bring this flavor potential to life. Mike was driven to find a cheese worthy of their milk. He decided he would have to become a cheesemaker himself to realize his milk's potential.

To find the cheese worthy of their (costly) efforts, Mike would engineer a business plan that would lead them to the right market. Once they understood that market, they could create the right cheese—a cheese that would reward them for the unusual qualities of their milk.

As part of his systematic research into the cheese market, Mike was learning that there might be a growing market for cheese that tastes really good. After all, craft beers and ten-dollar-a-pound coffee certainly pointed to a renewed interest among Americans in food that pleases.

In the late 1990s, Mike went to the American Cheese Society conference in Madison to scout out the geography of taste among sophisticated palates. (The ACS is an organization of cheesemakers and cheese enthusiasts that promotes taste as well as technique as an alternative to mass-market cheese. Flavor and distinctiveness rule.) As Mike notes,

> Our costs were going to be two, three, maybe four or five times what a small cheese factory's cost would be. And the only way that you can command a high price for cheese is to have just incredibly richly flavored cheese, a unique cheese that is not available other places. And then we decided that we would do everything we could possibly think of to pack flavor into this cheese, and we would not

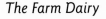

The Farm Dairy

Moving milk off the farm and into an industrial setting, whether cheese factory, creamery, condensery, or milk bottling plant, opened the floodgates to greater and greater production and prosperity for Wisconsin dairy farmers. Specialization of production freed farmers to concentrate on better and more productive care of their cows and allowed manufacturers to concentrate on quality and cost. This is why we call it the dairy *industry*.

However, for a long time many dairymen had no interest in passing the profits from processing their milk to the often-despised factoryman and the even-more-despised middleman (the cheese brokers and contract men), especially when there was a wife and daughters at home "willing" to work for nothing. Buttermaking was practiced at home until the 1920s and beyond, and farmer-owned milk routes were still a popular source of income for farmers near a town or city until the 1950s.

Cheesemaking was a different story, however, as making good cheese economically is a specialized skill requiring expensive equipment, buildings, and expertise. And making a cheese factory pay required the milk from enough cows—far more than any one farm could provide.

But farm dairies are making a comeback today, especially for farmers making

An early farm dairy and its unpaid employee

WHi Image ID 33519

cheeses they hope will transcend commodity status—and prices. Today's farm dairies have enough cows to make cheesemaking pay. For example, Saxon Homestead Creamery in Cleveland, Wisconsin, makes cheese from its 425 cows (see page 61). In the old days this would have represented thirty-five small farms with only twelve cows each.

In a way, the new farm dairies are becoming the crossroads cheese factories
continued ...

of today. The farmers building these factories are seeking greater profits, more independence and self-sufficiency, a larger scope for their managerial skills, a use for excess capital, and a sort of sense of completion—something they can hold and taste, something to complete the cycle from sunlight to pleasure on their own farms. They are, in short, yeoman-farmer-entrepreneurs.

The farm dairy—or "kitchen"—was often pictured as a place of great wholesomeness where women joyfully fed their families on the goodness of nature. This was contrasted, at least in the minds of the readers of the time, with the factory, the redoubt of money-minded factorymen.

Summer Sunshine in the Winter Churning

WHAT a satisfaction to take from the churn a mass of rich, golden butter, sweet as clover in spring, although the pastures are buried in snow! June triumphant over winter! The principle of conservation revealed in a homely but profitable commonplace. This is a daily experience on farms that are equipped with the

INDIANA SILO

By preserving the juices and fibers as well as the grains, retaining all the sugar and all the succulence that sunshine and rain have contributed to the growing plants, the Indiana Silo reproduces in the winter ration the qualities that give richness and abundance to the dairy yield. The air-tight walls of the Indiana Silo prevent mildew and so perfect is its protection that the heat developed in the curing silage prevents freezing, even in the coldest weather.

Write for Catalog, Booklet and Early Buyers' Money-Saving Proposition.

THE INDIANA SILO COMPANY, 515 Union Bldg., Anderson, Ind.
515 Live Stock Exch. Bldg., Kansas City, Mo.   515 Indiana Bldg., Des Moines ,Ia.
515 Live Stock Exch. Bldg., Fort Worth, Tex.

Successful Farming, February 1915

worry about what it cost, because we [felt] that the market would reward us . . . if we were successful and really putting a lot of flavor in the cheese.

So we decided we would only use a portion of our milk, which was that portion that would make the best flavored cheese. When our pastures are at their best is when we use that milk. May, June, early July—after that we are selective. When the rains are good, the pastures are good. So, we basically key it off the rain patterns, and we will make cheese for a week or two weeks straight in August, September, October and then stop if we don't have the right pasture conditions. We are very selective in the milk that we use, and we even size this operation to only use about half of our milk because we knew half of it . . . would not be the quality that we were looking for.

Mike worked with the University of Wisconsin Department of Dairy Science to create the right cheese for his market, a cheese that would take the greatest advantage of his and Dan's milk and their willingness to invest in taste. He settled on a French Alpine cheese called Beaufort. Traditional Beaufort is a raw milk cheese made from pasture-fed cows and aged with the labor-intensive wash-rind technique to slowly develop flavor. Mike would transform Beaufort into Gingrich and christen it Pleasant Ridge Reserve.

Mike made many experimental cheeses at the university's small-scale cheese plant and took them home to age in an ice chest in his basement in Dodgeville. As each cheese was ready he gathered friends and family for cheese klatches around his kitchen table. And thus Pleasant Ridge Reserve cheese—a cheese that is likely the most decorated cheese in the United States—was born by the "mmmmms" and "aahhs" of Wisconsinites.

Mike's business strategy was to enter the fine food world and win the palates of taste-setters around the country. To do so, he would have to enter his cheese in highly competitive arenas.

In 2001 he decided to put his toe in the water at the American Cheese Society's competition in the "Farmstead" class, with its smaller number of entrants and lower status in the eyes of the industry, rather than going head-to-head against the best. He would be most happy if he could win in that category. In the end, his cheese stood alone. Pleasant Ridge Reserve won Best of Show despite Mike's modest expectations.

Pleasant Ridge was named U.S. Champion Cheese at the technically oriented U.S. Championship Cheese Contest in 2003 and took Best of Show in the American Cheese Society competition again in 2005. Remarkably, Pleasant Ridge is the only cheese to win top honors in both contests, demonstrating both a mastery of flavor and a mastery of technique. Not bad for a former Whole-Earther and a corporate dropout.

In 2007 Mike's cheese won the Gallo Gold Medal for artisanal dairy products, placing it among the finest cheeses made in America—and making it one of the most sought-after cheeses in the finest restaurants in New York, San Francisco, and Chicago.

You might say that Pleasant Ridge Reserve has become the poster cheese for the American renaissance in fine foods. This is a turn of events that Mike and Dan, in their understated Midwestern way, did not expect. After all, they set out to be dairy farmers and earn a living caring among cows. As Mike puts it:

I am just amazed that this cheese is as well known as it is all around the country. I mean, I hear from people who have had it in some big city someplace and have recognized it. It has a national reputation—now that really has surprised me that it has been able to do as well as it has. I did not think that we would get this big. We are still quite small in the cheese world, but we are

About Mike, his wife, Carol, says, "I wish [everyone] would appreciate the fact that he has put himself into this cheese. . . . He does not skimp, he does not change things, he does everything to make it as good as it could possibly be. It is an honest cheese."

making about 60,000 pounds a year, which is more than I would have thought we would get to.

Rather than the seventeen dollars per hundredweight they would have gotten if they just waved good-bye to their milk at their farm gate, Mike and Dan now get something like one hundred dollars per hundredweight for their milk sold in the form of cheese. And they receive something quite priceless as well: the appreciation of sophisticated people who have tasted this product of *their* land, *their* cows, *their* values, and the work of *their* hands.

So what do you get when you cross a progressive conservative philosopher and an engineer in Wisconsin? A blue-ribbon cheese and a prosperous farm, of course.

And you get a new model for young dairy farmers who wish to be among cows without squeezing too much out of nature—or themselves.

The Mayers of Slinger: a dairy family

A Dairy Farm Family

⌇

THE MAYERS

It's what makes you get out of bed in the morning, regardless
of the milk price being high or being low, or the rain being right,
or the sun being too low, it is that miracle the first time that you
get to see a calf take its feet. You can watch that over and
over again—the rebirth. —Shelly Mayer

I MET SHELLY MAYER in the office above her family's white barn, surrounded by piles of farm records dating back one hundred years. We chatted while a dozen screeching palm-sized kittens demanded her attention and scurried under my feet.

Hanging on the wall were blue ribbons from state fairs past and pictures of the Mayers and their prized cows. The century's worth of yellowing bits and pieces of the history of people who learned to care for cows mixed with the atmosphere of living dairying: cow smells and sounds from the barn below, where Shelly's husband, Ike, her son, Devin, and Ike's brother, Dennis, were milking.

Unlike the office above, there is little chaos in the barn below. Cows take their places to be milked under the direction of an unseen choreographer, a kind of bovine Busby Berkeley directing a chorus line of not particularly graceful dancers.

In Ike Mayer's barn, cows are in their stanchions, manure is plopping into the gutter, and milk is surging through the pipe. This means all is right in the world for Ike Mayer, because Ike likes working with cows "more than I like working with people." The

The Mayers have been interested in cows for a long time. These same ribbons deck the walls of the family's barn today, along with many newer ones. The gentleman in the center—the one with the huge smile—is the grandfather of the present inhabitant of the Mayers' barn, Ike.

satisfying wordless order of his barn is testimony to his modest and happy relationship with his cows. Ike Mayer *is* a dairyman.

I met Ike's father, seventy-two-year-old Dick Mayer, at Shelly and Ike's kitchen table overlooking their barn only fifty yards away. That barn is the place where Dick milked and bred prize-winning cows for fifty years. Dick Mayer believes, I think, that being a dairy farmer is the best thing a person could do in life. "Our three oldest children all married farmers or farmers' daughters," he proclaims with pride. "And they're still farming." The Mayers of Slinger have made dairy farming something to be proud of.

While the deep dairy smells of silage, ground corn, hay, and cow predominate on this forty-acre, seventy-cow farm, there is something else in the air here. It may be the faint whiff of sadness, because Milwaukee is only a half-hour drive away for the new residents of rural Slinger in their five-acre, three-car-garage homes standing on land that once supported cows. The Mayers live on a kind of dairy island no longer embraced by 360 degrees of Dairyland. On this island dairying is practiced in a way that would be familiar to past generations of Mayers, who practiced it here for one hundred years. But that way may be fading. Their story has a note of poignancy in it. But it also has an awful lot of heart in it—the dairy farmer's heart, still beating after all these years.

Ike, Shelly, and Dick are very different people, to be sure. But they are bound strongly by their passion. They love working with cows, and they really like to apply their "eye for cattle" to develop more-perfect cows, cows that they and others want to have in their barn. And they like to profit from their skills. They have profited from improvement for many years.

This is the story of a family united in their diversity by the joys, satisfactions, frustrations, hard times, and profits of animal husbandry and the dignity of its professional calling. This is the story of a venerable dairy family in a changing world.

The Mayers started out in Wisconsin in 1849, immigrants in search of land, prosperity, and freedom. By the turn of the century, Mayers were "interested in cows." They began buying registered cows, hitching their wagon to the rising star of improved dairying and the ascendancy of purebred Holstein cows.

Mayers became interested in improved dairying around the time Dick's father enrolled in the dairy short courses at the University of Wisconsin as an eighteen-year-old in 1918. There he joined other young farmers taken with the idea that learning and science could

Courtesy of the Mayer family

Dick Mayer doing
what he loved best,
showing cows

improve the lives of farmers. For fifty-four years Dick's father, Christian, was on the board of directors of the Washington County Dairy Herd Improvement Association, so committed was he to the great idea of improvement—and to the market value of selling improvement.

There is much to tell about Dick Mayer: about his trips to Mexico to sell prize-winning cattle and his many trips to the winner's circle at dairy competitions around the country. And the profits he made by selling cows and bulls others wanted. And about his decades-long work as an official dairy cow judge and the many young people he tutored in the finer points of dairy form and function. About how he spent many, many hours with farm children teaching them how to present themselves with confidence, dignity, and pride in the show ring. Dick Mayer is a man who has been interested in the improvement of farmers as well as their livestock.

Ike Mayer is in the middle of his life. He is the father of three, a graduate of the University of Wisconsin, and owner, along with his wife, Shelly, of an average-sized herd of about seventy cows. He milks three times a day in a white, tie-stanchion barn with his brother and his son Devin, when Devin is not away at the university.

Ike and Shelly own just forty acres now and rent twenty more, the price of land being too high to afford to maintain the hundreds of acres the Mayer family once had. Besides, Ike really dislikes machinery and is mostly glad he can buy his feed from others.

Ike Mayer is a "good cow man" (a badge pinned on him by his father) and a hands-on dairyman of the old order. He simply enjoys being among cows in the companionable familiarity of the barn with its timeless rituals and order. I joined him and his brother there for the second of their three daily milkings.

Improving Dairy Cows through Intelligent Design

For progressive dairy farmers, managing the improvement of their herds is one of their most intellectually enjoyable occupations. Indeed, improvement through intelligent design is one of the tenets of the progressive movement itself. Seeing their herd become more and more productive over the course of a career is one of the ways dairy farmers measure themselves and one of the professional rewards of being in dairying.

And in an industry in which profit margins are constantly squeezed, managing for improvement is one of the most important dairy survival skills. Cows that produce calves and milk for as long as possible are cows worth feeding.

Since the beginning of commercial dairying as a way to improve farmers' lives, dairypeople have been exhorted to eliminate "boarder" cows from their herds— that is, to feed only cows that proved to be profitable over the long run. The science of profitable cows has become extraordinarily more sophisticated, data driven, and effective since the days when huge udders and seven-day milk records were considered the mark of a great cow.

To simplify a highly complex intellectual activity: dairy farmers can use two basic "tools" to accomplish their improvement goals. They can breed their cows

ROMPING of C.N. 64860.   LITHO DEPT, INTERNATIONAL STOCK FOOD @
PROFITABLE FOR YOUR MILK COWS.
27

Hoard's Dairyman, March 16, 1906

It is likely that Romping of C.N.'s offspring are still producing prodigious amounts of milk today in Wisconsin dairy barns. The great cows of Wisconsin have contributed much to our state and ought to be honored in the Capitol.

to bulls who are proved to effect some important characteristic in their daughters, such as udder placement or strong hoofs, and they can eliminate cows at the tail end of their herd's bell curve for such sins as being difficult to get pregnant regularly. In other words, herds are improved through inheritance and, most effectively, through selection.

(*Selection* is of course a euphemism for sending a cow to her demise, which is a euphemism for killing her. For many

continued . . .

These herdsmen at the Crave brothers' farm in Waterloo are meeting to discuss the improvement of a dairy herd in Wisconsin. For the uninitiated these meetings would sound as though they were being conducted in ancient Sumerian, so arcane and specialized is the language. But it is in meetings like these that Wisconsin's agricultural competitiveness is maintained.

Photo by Mark Henrichs

dairy farmers, though not for all, this is a sad reality of their way of life. I always found it wrenching but necessary. When my son was four he once asked, "Where is Number 12 going?" as she was loaded onto the truck to take her to slaughter. "She's going to Dubuque," was my answer. In our family "going to Dubuque" means, well . . . you know, going to Dubuque.)

Over the years, the definition of what are important traits in a dairy cow has changed, as has the science of what can and cannot be inherited. Likewise, our understanding of what makes a cow valuable has changed and deepened as well.

What has not changed, at least among progressive dairy farmers, is their deep interest in improving what they start with and in leaving their children with a more valuable herd of dairy cows. Dairy farmers enjoy the intelligence of design.

Hanging out with Ike in his barn while he milks is to be with a man who is at home. His movements, as he goes from cow to cow, are graceful, economic, practiced, and purposeful. This somewhat-reticent man becomes animated as he talks with professional ease about his cows and the business of caring for them, his words flowing as fluidly as his movements as he goes about his business. As he massages one cow's udder, puts the teat cups on another, or takes them off a third, he instructs me on the composition of a dairy ration, the value of strong legs, and the proper placement of the udder. I am instructed in the fundamental teachings of an ancient craft in Ike's barn, where all is well with the world.

But outside, the always-changing world of dairy economics and the march of human progress is putting pressure on full-contact dairymen like Ike Mayer to add "cow numbers." The small profit that each cow provides too often does not add up to what it takes to raise and educate a family today.

Unfortunately for dairy farmers like Ike, adding more cows means adding people and managing humans rather than cows, something that quiet cow-men would like to avoid. Ike wants to continue "doing the thing I want to do, the way I'm doing it right here" until he retires.

IKE MET SHELLY KELLER in the show ring at the junior state fair. Shelly was *not* one of those farm kids who couldn't wait to get off the farm, one of those kids who would never, ever marry a farmer. She was one of those kids who was deeply connected to living things. "If it had four legs and a heartbeat," her father told her, "you would fall in love with it."

As a small child in Richland County, Shelly Keller fell in love with miracles as practiced on Wisconsin dairy farms. And like so many other Wisconsin farm children, she became deeply attached to rebirth. She remembers,

> We had a cow that was getting ready to deliver a calf. And my grandma was with me, and I was maybe four years old. And I remember

Courtesy of the Mayer family

grandma saying to me, "You know, Shelly, out of all my years and all the things I've witnessed, still I think the neatest thing is the first time a calf finds its feet."

Out of all the miracles that we have a chance to work with in the dairy business, still one of the coolest and neatest things—and it's what makes you get out of bed in the morning, regardless of the milk price being high or being low, or the rain being right, or the sun being too low, it is that miracle the first time that you get to see a calf take its feet. You can watch that over and over again—the rebirth.

It is, she says, "the simple things," the "things that get you out of bed in the morning," that are at the heart of her and Ike's passion for dairying.

Grandma Keller, Shelly Mayer's grandmother and instructor in dairy miracles

In our worst of times, our most difficult economic times since we've bought the farm, I looked at my husband and said, "You know, we both have degrees from the university, so it's not like we have to do this. We chose this career." And I've looked at him a multitude of times, usually when he's frustrated, I'll try to focus him, I'll say, "What do you want to do? You don't look happy. What do you want to do?"

He goes, "There's nothing I want to do other than farm."

We chose a business that we knew we loved because we grew up in it. Dairying is a good way of life. You've got that connectedness with the land. You love being outside. You love working with animals. Maybe we're spoiled, because I don't know if everybody wakes up in the morning and says, "I love what I do."

Do we love every part of it? No! I don't like cold weather. I don't like frozen water pipes. I don't like low milk prices and struggling.

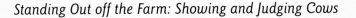

Standing Out off the Farm: Showing and Judging Cows

It is not always easy to be recognized for doing things well on the farm. After all, many farmers are isolated from their neighbors, spending their days doing chores. Certainly a handsome house—maybe one a little bigger than the neighbors'—with good fences and well-painted barns shows a farmer's face to the world in a good light. A big tractor and well-cultivated fields help as well. It is just that so much of what a farmer does is done with no one around to see how well he or she is doing it.

But since the beginning of dairying, the show ring and dairy judging have been among the few arenas where a dairy farmer young or old could stand out, be seen, and earn praise.

While showing cows is, of course, about showing off cows for fun and profit, it is just as much about showing *oneself*. Poise, dignity, and good grooming—for cow and human—are virtues rewarded in the show ring. Making a name is good business both for those selling breeding stock and for those selling themselves. The show ring is a public place where a human can be judged in the eyes of the dairy world.

Competitive dairy judging is a somewhat arcane sport where the dairy farmer's art of understanding the relationship between bovine form and function has long been taught. Learning to see cows through the eyes of experts has offered ambitious

continued . . .

Ike Mayer (center) has been a "good cow man," as his father says, ever since he was a boy. In being recognized by the dairy cognoscenti at an early age, young farmers like Ike Mayer are accepted into the fellowship of serious dairy farmers.

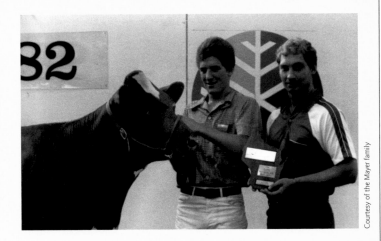

Courtesy of the Mayer family

Like Ike Mayer, Shelly Keller was recognized at an early age for her success in the show ring. In fact, she and Ike found each other at a Holstein show and were able to marry within the dairy faith. And so dairying goes forward into succeeding generations.

Courtesy of the Mayer family

young people the chance to participate in the progressive development of "the breed." It helps initiate them into the lodge of serious dairymen.

Showing and judging are also social experiences, for young people especially, and one of the great sources for the circulation of better farming practices. These events also no doubt introduce farmer boy to farmer girl. It allows them, if they wish, to marry within the faith. This may explain why dairying seems to run in families. It certainly keeps families on the land.

Dairying is a good way of life, but it's got to be a profitable way of life. Otherwise, it's not romantic at all.

Everything has to be in check and balance. So it's that passion that gets you through the low times; it's the professionalism and the business skills that makes it a good way of life.

Making farming a profession has been the mission of progressive dairying from the beginning, and Shelly Mayer is one of those true Wisconsin progressive dairy farmers for whom the great Idea of Dairying itself is as important as their own cows or blue ribbons. The

A yeoman-farmer cat

dairy industry to these men and women is the bulwark that protects the miracles and way of life they love.

But the miracles that can make dairying spiritually rewarding must be paid for with the same coin we all use to pay our way in life.

To many progressive dairy farm leaders like Shelly Mayer, asserting their right to be prosperous is what is necessary for farmers to survive. *Profit* is not a four-letter word to them, because profits protect the deep moral core they see at the center of Wisconsin dairying: care of the cow and the soil that feeds her. Shelly says,

> You know, we and the kids will talk about our love for working with cattle. Our kids do love their cows, but they understand that they're not human. In this small family farm, cows are, when it comes down to it, production units. And that's the reality of it and how we have to look at it.
>
> But that doesn't mean that we look at that animal as being disposable and having only a financial worth. And I can't speak for other dairymen, I can only speak for what drives us to spend that extra hour, or if need be, that extra eight hours by an animal to get them through. If [our daughter] Cassie's calves look at her wrong,

"The Cow a Manufacturer.—Some writers object to a cow being called a machine, but I think it makes little difference whether we call her a machine, a converter, a condenser or some other name; but it makes a great difference how we feed and care for her. Whatever we call her, she manufactures our coarse fodder and grain into milk and we should do our part well to aid her in performing this work to our profit. She requires a certain amount to keep herself in working order and our share comes after she has taken care of herself, and whether or not our share is sufficient to make us a profit depends many times on the way we have cared for and fed her."

—H. B. Gurler, *The Farm Dairy*, 1908

A meeting of the Bashaw Valley Farmers Club in an undated picture. Farmers have always been keen on educating themselves and their neighbors in the ways of progress.

and if she thinks they're going to get a runny nose, she goes out of her way to make sure that they get extra bedding to lie on. Or she'll check them during the night. It's going above and beyond.

Do I worry about this business becoming too much mechanical? No, because a cow is only going to give back to man what man gives them. A cow that's well taken care of is going to take care of the person who takes care of her. So those who are going to survive and thrive and have a legacy to pass on in the dairy business are going to be the people who run it like a business but are still in tune with the animal.

In the early days of the dairy industry, the progressive leadership worked to convince farmers that they could think of themselves as professionals if they thought *like* professionals. Besides working alongside Ike on their farm, Shelly is the executive director of the Professional Dairy Producers of Wisconsin, an organization, similar to the influential, farmer-run Farmers' Institutes of the 1880s, that is all about helping farmers think through every aspect of the business of caring for cows and themselves.

So, while her husband cares for their cows, Shelly cares for her fellow dairy farmers.

For one hundred years, the Mayers of Slinger have learned to keep body and soul together by caring for cows. They have found ways to make getting up in the morning worthwhile and sometimes even joyful. They have weathered many, many difficulties by daily readings from the gospel of miracles and profits that is the book of dairying in Wisconsin. They are together today, bound by their passion, a Wisconsin dairy farm family.

A view of the Iversons' farm: their home

Beauty in the Barn

꒱

HANNAH IVERSON AND FAMILY

*A couple of years ago my brother bought a Guernsey, and I
decided that if my brother could have a Guernsey, I needed one,
too. I went and I bought my Guernsey and I started working with
her and she calved in, and every time she calved in she had a heifer.
So now I have this cow with four calves; we've never had a bull.
Then I thought, well, I'll take her to Madison. I took her to
[World Dairy] Expo last fall, and she stood second
in the junior show.* —Hannah Iverson

DENNIS AND NANCY IVERSON are valley farmers who you just know
have earned their happiness the old-fashioned way.

Their farm defines "nestled." To get there you drive a mile back
from the county highway along a gravel road. At the cul du sac of their
lush valley, with its corn standing at attention like rows of ancient
Chinese terra-cotta soldiers, you will find their modest farm with two
homes, a red barn, two open-air barns for their calves, and heifers.

And here you will find Hannah, unless she's at the university in
Platteville. Hannah is a farm girl from a small valley who is on her
way to the larger arenas of dairying, the daughter of a small red barn,
a young woman with big ideas.

At eighteen Hannah was named the Wisconsin Young Entrepreneur of the Year. She was the 2008 National Guernsey Princess.
And she is an aspiring Guernsey breeder and an agricultural entrepreneur. She is a young woman who will make much of herself.

The Iverson farm around the 1920s. The barn and home still house Iversons and their cows.

"In rural life, however tame and lonely, the home is not merely a few square feet hedged in by brick walls, but the whole wide countryside: the barns, the fields, the woods, the orchards, the animals wild and domesticated, the outlook over hill and valley—these all constitute the farmer's home."

—Isaac Phillips Roberts, *The Farmstead*, 1900

As Hannah was coming down from the barn to meet me, her father, Dennis, let me in on something that is very important to him and Nancy and their happiness: it seems that in the 1940s Dennis's grandfather had a well-known, respected, and profitable herd of registered Guernseys on this isolated valley farm. Soon, Dennis believes, his daughter will have a well-known, respected, and profitable herd of registered Guernseys here, too. As Nancy says, "We can do it again; there's no reason we can't have top cattle here again."

Because of their daughter's ability to see beyond their small farm into the much larger world of dairying, a new world is opening up to the Iversons beyond the sometimes-closed—and at times confining—universe of the barn and the daily and seasonal rituals of dairying. Today the Iversons are seeing their herd grow more beautiful and win blue ribbons under Hannah's

Hannah and her family: brother Nathan, father Dennis, mother Nancy, and grandfather Alvin

guidance. They are watching udders shape up, backs straighten, and heads being held higher. They are seeing cows becoming more perfect expressions of that Platonic form called "dairy cow." Hannah's more beautiful cows now add a new grace note to the day-to-day life of the Iversons, grace that both pleases and, they hope, profits them. Beauty in the barn changes things.

The beauty and notoriety of Hannah's cows will increase their value. With increased value and notoriety come increased pride. Hannah is bringing pride to her family, and with that pride has come the happiness-producing idea that things can be different, better, easier, and more satisfying on their farm. This is a great balm to small farmers too often battered by low prices, bad weather, monotony, and anonymity.

Hannah Iverson is a young woman who means business. She is both ambitious and in love with all things dairy. And she wants to stand out:

> I've been involved in dairy judging since I was little. I started show-
> ing when I was in second grade, at our county fair. I guess Mom

Getting dairy farmers
to appreciate individual
animals and to find plea-
sure in them was part of
the effort to raise dairying up from drudgery to
a humanistic occupation
that rewarded farmers
with "higher" pleasures.

THE QUEEN OF THE DAIRY

By EDGAR L. VINCENT

Successful Farming, December 1914

said that I caught the fever from there. I just started getting more involved in going to various seminars and clinics to learn what you need to do to compete successfully in a show ring. From there I started going to the spring shows and the summer show and then eventually World Dairy Expo. I started going down there when I was in seventh grade with a friend. I love showing cattle. I love getting them ready and going in the ring. I think what I love the most about it is seeing your hard work pay off.

On a small forty-cow farm like the Iversons', there is plenty of hard work to be sure. But sometimes there just isn't quite enough payoff.

Certainly there are many inherent rewards that come from living the rhythms of nature and of cows. It's just that this life is also very demanding, allowing little extra energy that can be invested in the day after tomorrow. Keeping things going on a small farm can be enough: calves require pretty constant care and plenty of anxiety about keeping up "cow numbers" so the barn is full and the milk check doesn't shrink. Cows get sick, and sometimes it seems it is always the best ones that die. Putting up enough good forage and grain is a sunup to sunset occupation in the spring and summer, work often ruined by weather that is indifferent to farmers' hopes. The barn must be cleaned and manure dealt with every day. Cows must be milked two or even three times a day and the milk line and tank cleaned. And things always need

repairing, all the time, no matter the minus degrees of winter. Then, of course, there's the yard.

Of course, doing the chores can be comfortable, familiar, and even nourishing. As Nancy puts it:

> When nobody's home and I'm in the barn by myself, in the morning, that's my favorite time. Because it's not real challenging work. So you can milk the cows and you can plan what you need to do. It's your time by yourself. And it's just great.

But those rewards aren't always great enough. Enter Hannah and her Classic View Enterprise, and Blenda, her prize-winning Guernsey.

Having beautiful cows like Blenda in a barn makes dairying more pleasurable, adding a grace note to an occupation often mired in routine and manure. The dairy farmer's day, as is true for everyone else, is made happier in the presence of beauty. Aesthetics in dairying is an important factor in keeping people on the farm.

Hannah and her grand-father Alvin, a dairyman of the old school. For thirty years Alvin commuted daily to the Twin Cities for a job in a factory. He farmed in the morning, in the evening, and on weekends with his son Dennis. Today he supervises all aspects of the farm and keeps the past bound with the present for the Iversons.

Photo by Mark Fay

When she was in fifth grade Hannah bought her first calf for four hundred dollars. A few years later, with a five-thousand-dollar loan from a farm youth program, she started buying registered cows for her own herd.

Today Hannah has twenty cows and heifers, a herd within her parents' herd. In exchange for her labor on their farm, Dennis and Nancy feed and house Hannah's cows, forwarding to Hannah her portion of the milk check. But Hannah is not in the milk business. She sells genetics. She sells potential. She sells Blenda's status and her own personality.

My original goal was: I wanted to be a farmer, and I wanted to milk cows. Then I started building my herd and milking cows, and then

160　CREATING DAIRYLAND

I started getting involved with the other aspects of the dairy industry, showing and marketing and all the other fun stuff. Then I had a chance to serve as the Guernsey Princess, and I love getting out there and meeting people and networking and communicating—which essentially helps you build your business.

Hannah's business, and her real passion, is heifer calves: nature's own reward for being a dairy farmer. She explains,

A wonderful day of my life on the farm? That would have to be when I get a heifer calf. You're always waiting nine months to see if your hard work pays off. So that day when the calf is finally born, and it's a heifer, it's amazing because you know that you have the money from her. It makes for a good day. Wow! I finally got something.

I stand in the barn and I admire [a new heifer] and I think, two years from now she's going to be standing next to her mom, hopefully. I want to watch them grow and see how they develop. It's fun to see what they grow into and see how the sire selection has improved the genetics from dam to daughter. This past October my cow won second [at World Dairy Expo] and she also won the genetic merit award. So she had, I guess, the best genetics in the class. That's so exciting for us. Just to have that positive feedback that we're doing something right.

If I hadn't gotten involved we'd still be just milking cows. We're not. We're looking towards the genetic end of things in the future now.

DENNIS IVERSON is a dairy farmer with strictly working-class cows. Like so many other farmers, Dennis once measured his accomplishments by "how much work I could get done in a day." Like their cows, they are blue collar—farmers, not businesspeople, content to do an honest day's work, have a cup of coffee with the buddies in town after evening milking, and wait for the milk check at the end of the month. Once in a while, they have enough to buy a new piece of equipment to make their work just a bit easier as they get older.

The Motherhood Business

Dairy farming is about pregnancy, maternity, and, if I may speak freely, the act that precedes pregnancy.

Managing the timely and successful breeding of a herd of dairy cows is one of the most important and challenging tasks for dairy farmers. To be profitable, they must effectively manage the sexual lives of their cows so they will be in peak milk production as much as possible over the course of their lives.

In a modern high-producing herd, a cow should calve every twelve and a half to thirteen months. The longer she is "open"—not bred back after her milk production has peaked—the less milk she will be able to give over her lifetime.

Keeping this open period as short as possible is a very important management task. Dairy farmers wish to minimize inseminations in order to save money and to get the cow back on the mommy track as quickly as possible.

Therefore, knowing when his or her cows are sexually receptive—in heat—is one of the most important pieces of intelligence a dairy herd manager must have. The period in which a cow is in heat lasts from six to thirty hours only. If one heat goes by undetected, it will be eighteen to twenty-four days before the next. Therefore, dairy famers keep extensive records in order to predict a cow's heat and her future calving dates.

"Motherhood and mother-love are the very foundation of the dairy industry. When a man comes to look upon a cow as a mother, a calf as a baby and young stock as growing children, he is in a very fair way to learn how to handle them." —R. M. Washburn, *Productive Dairying,* 1917

© Wisconsin Milk Marketing Board, Inc.

And because it takes on average 1.7 "services"—or insemination events—to get a dairy cow pregnant, knowing that a cow is pregnant after service is also hugely important.

Today the vast majority of breeding takes place through artificial insemination (AI). Farmers are reluctant to keep bulls on their farms because they are dangerous and because doing so limits the genetic pool available to their cows. But without a bull to sniff out a receptive cow, dairy farmers must substitute skill, science, and effort.

The most obvious way for a dairy farmer to detect heat is through cow-on-cow sexual activity. *Mounting* is the term of art. Dairy farmers spend as much time as possible closely watching their herds during the times their cows are free to mingle with each other. While the cows go out to the yard, a farmer will stand at the fence scanning and watching for the tell-tale signs of heat so she or he can have the cow serviced within the short window of opportunity. Because cows spend so much time away from the farmer, it is easy to miss these events. (Seventy percent of mounting takes place between 7:00 at night and 7:00 in the morning.)

Today's progressive farmers use modern technology and biochemistry to make breeding less chancy. In one method, a small, pressure-sensitive device is attached to a potentially receptive cow. This device includes a wireless transmitter

Photo by Mark Henrichs

Rebirth—the dairy farmer's joy!

that reports directly to the herdsman's computer. A "You've Got Male" message is received, and the inseminator is dispatched to cow number 1856.

Artificial insemination involves an inseminator, a gloved arm, an injector, and the "genetics" from a chosen bull. It is a rather clinical affair.

Cows who have a history of being difficult to breed are on the bubble, life-and-death-wise. Knowing if a cow has conceived is so important that many modern dairy farmers pay for the vet to come out to perform ultrasound or other tests for pregnancy.

The great wheel of new birth must be kept rolling.

Perhaps at some point they can just sit back and watch life go by without having to work at it.

For men like Dennis, registered cattle were a kind of frivolity of the upper classes, like cows modeling in the pages of slick fashion magazines. They had nothing to do with the work of the farm. He says,

> I never used to think much of these registered cattle. I always thought, well this two to three thousand dollar register cow doesn't give any more milk than my one thousand dollar–grade cow. But [I wasn't] realizing what you can do with the genetics with the registered cattle through breeding. Hannah's basically taught me that if you really put a herd together, the milk will be the by-product. The genetics will be what makes you the money. Because I would have never dreamt that we would be selling registered stock—anything like this.
>
> I'm not going to study the genetics like my wife and daughter are. They'll sit there with the catalogs on these bulls and dams and stuff, and study them for hours. I'm probably sitting at the computer playing solitaire. I might be in town having coffee.

Hannah and her mother understand the work of a dairy farm in a different way. To them the goal of all their effort is to excel by increasing the value of what you start with. As Nancy puts it:

> If you want to set an example for your children, you have to say, okay, this calf is okay, but we can tweak it a little bit, we can use genetics, we can improve a little bit. And what I love about it is, it's always, "Wait till the next one. Wait till the next calf comes. That one's going to really be nice." And we would one day like to breed one of the top cows. And people say, "Ho, that's a high goal." That's okay. You have to keep reaching and keep setting more goals for yourself.

Recently Hannah entered the embryo transfer (ET) business as a way to increase the value of her best cows. While her fees are modest (only two hundred dollars for each embryo), the business is a new source of income and recognition. "That two hundred dollars," Hannah says, "makes me happy."

Today many things on the Iversons' newly looking-to-the-future farm make them happy: Hannah's success in the larger world, to be sure; her remaking of their herd into a troupe of more graceful performers; and the prospects of greater income.

Dennis and Nancy Iverson have earned their happiness the old-fashioned way: by hard honest work with earth, animals, and weather; through difficult times, calves being born, the best cows dying; and through faith in all manner of things—especially the faith that their children's lives will be better than theirs.

Photo by Jerry Quebe

I hope that when you pass fallen-down barns and deserted farmsteads like this one in Crawford County, you will sense at least that a dairy story was lived there once. Each of these, as T. S. Eliot said, "marks a place where a story ended." Stories that end can be as interesting as stories that continue—but sometimes they're harder to read.

A Place Where a Story Ended

⌇

WILLIAM SEELY

My father sat in the evenings and read the newspaper.
He knew about rotating crops and things like that [but he
didn't have] a silo. I think my father, having given up his own
life, did what he had to do and that was all he could manage. . . .
But [he said], "I learned to love the land." I can only guess what
he meant, but you know, he came to that sort of relationship
with the beauty of his surroundings. He took what
he could. —Mae Seely Sylvester

LOOKING TOWARD THE WISCONSIN RIVER from Highway 60 a few miles west of Wauzeka, you will enjoy a view of open wetlands, rushes and ducks, geese, and all manner of things that don't need mankind to flourish.

But this land was once a farm. It was owned by William James Seely, a man who toiled here with a heavy heart. William Seely was a reluctant farmer. This land, now so unmarked by man, also marks the place where a dairy story ended.

For this, like many thousands of similar places in Wisconsin, is a place where the joys of farming were not sufficient. The story of William Seely and his children is perhaps the most common story in Dairyland, for it is the story of how grazing cows, warm milk, pungent barns, straining horses, and all manner of things just "didn't pay." William Seely is long gone to the earth, as is his farm, but his daughter, Mae, is left to tell his story.

William Seely's farm before it returned to nature

My father did not intend to be a farmer. And in a very real sense, [he] wasn't. That was not the life he would have chosen for himself. My father joined the navy just out of high school during World War I. He did basic training at the Great Lakes Training Center in Chicago. So when he was discharged, he went to Chicago to live. And he got a job in the post office there. And he was living quite happily in Chicago and loved Chicago. He was a Cubs fan. [He] loved to swim off the Oak Street Beach. He was having a good time. He was obviously drawn to a larger world.

Then his mother wrote and asked him to come home because his father was having heart problems. And after a very agonizing decision, he did that. My father was a city guy. It hurt him terribly. And it hurt all of us. So there were silences. Because there was in my father this terrible loss of his life, really.

He told me this on the day he and my mother moved from the farm. He and I walked to the pasture. [We] sat under the hickory trees, and out of his mouth came this story from I don't know where. But he told me exactly the story of his coming back to the farm, and how he had promised himself he was never going to do that. He came back because he decided that he had to come back.

William Seely, U.S.
Navy, circa 1917

Courtesy of Mae Seely Sylvester

An unidentified Wisconsin dairy farmer uses his back, circa 1940. Dairy farming, especially in the good old days, was an arm-hurting, back-bending occupation in which men were often reminded that on earth overcoming gravity takes some doing. Being sore at the end of the day—and at the end of a life—was one of the things that reminded farmers of how they had earned their livings. Mae Seely Sylvester says, "I have vivid memories of my father. He had a little cart that he would put milk cans in and lean into the weight up the incline to the windmill and the cooling tank. Then he would lift—my father was not a big man—he would lift these heavy steel cans full of milk, like about three feet to the lip of the cooling tank and then lower them in."

So he told me this story, and then he said, "But I learned to love the land." I can only guess what he meant, but you know, he came to that sort of relationship with the beauty of his surroundings. He took what he could.

My dad was a very tenderhearted guy. Whenever we had a litter of pigs there would always be a runt, and Dad would bring the runt into the house. And we would take care of it. It would sleep behind the wood stove in a box. And we would all feed it by hand with a little doll nipple kind of thing. And we would all love this pig. Of course we produced all our own food. How he ever brought himself to butcher a pig, I'll never know.

It took much brute doing to drag heavy chains through the mud, by yourself, to rescue a mired team or to place yourself between bickering Holsteins in a hundred-degree barn. It took much doing to cut hay all day, fork it onto a wagon, and heft it into the barn. For a man who, as Mae describes him, "roamed the farm quoting Longfellow and Whittier," too little poetry was to be found in field or barn.

My father sat in the evenings and read the newspaper. He knew about rotating crops and things like that [but he didn't have] a silo. I think my father, having given up his own life, did what he had to do and that was all he could manage.

Was it any wonder that men like William Seely had little interest in investing their hearts, minds, and meager resources in building up a farm? They were sworn to effect their children's escapes.

"I can't remember a time," Mae now says, "when I didn't know I would leave. It just wasn't enough. It wasn't enough."

Not enough to be sure. But as this sixty-eight-year-old professional woman has begun to discover, it was something—something important. Today on her desk at the University of Minnesota Medical School is a glass cow and this quote from the poet T. S. Eliot:

We shall not cease from exploration
And the end of all our exploring
Will be to arrive where we started
And know the place for the first time.

Mae returns in her mind to the cow paths of girlhood, the place she began.

> It was a sensual potpourri . . . I would go barefoot, and the paths, of course, were ground velvet [by] the cows' hoofs. So it was a delicious feeling walking along those paths. I would move through the pasture where the smells were a mixture of the cut alfalfa from the field, the various wild vegetation in the pasture. The hickory trees. And then of course there was the river and the slopes going down to it. The grasses. Raspberry patches here and there. And I can feel the heat of the summer. The cows always went to the farthest end of the pasture late in the day.
>
> It was always a kind of mystical thing to me that the cows—I felt connected to them, because I saw their intelligence in that they knew which stanchion was theirs. How much different could they be? You learn that kind of affinity as well as a reciprocity. That which sustains us is something to which we must give care.

"The census report does not give the number or value of the great men and noble women which the rural homes have produced, though they are the most valuable product of the farms. It says nothing about the perennial rural springs from which flow, in a never-ending stream, statesmen, divines, missionaries, teachers, students and business men. Although more than half of these life-giving energies of the nation and civilization come directly from the rural homes, the census report gives no clue by which the value of these, the nation's wealth and power, can be ascertained."

—Isaac Phillips Roberts, *The Farmstead*, 1900

This picture of Mae and Brownie allows Mae to return to the place where she began.

I didn't find milking pleasant. I didn't. Being tucked under the belly of a musky cow was not my idea of what I should be doing. But it needed to be done. And it was a part of our livelihood, and I was a part of that family. So I learned that there are things that you don't like doing that need to be done and that you need to do.

SINCE THE TIME when people started taking cows seriously in Wisconsin, we have produced butter and cheese almost beyond counting. We have re-created the land itself and have found ways to keep men and women happy on the farm. But our failure to keep some people on the land may be just as important a story. Our dairy farms have sent countless men and women out into the world, men

WILLIAM SEELY   173

Caleb Janus feeds Dennis the lamb on our Soldier's Grove farm in 1974. As A. J. Philips wrote in *Queen Vashti: The Autobiography of a Guernsey Cow*: "The easiest thing in the world is to train a child so it will be considerate of the rights of birds and beasts, and a child trained in that way is safe. When he is grown he will be considerate of the rights of men."

and women learned in the ways of caring, stalwart in their duties to what must be done, and firm in their connection to the natural world. Our dairy farms have produced countless worthy people. This, too, is part of the great success story of dairying in Wisconsin.

There are many places in Dairyland where a story ended, places where men like William Seely were reluctant, even unhappy, farmers. There are many places where boys and girls grew to love books, music, and adventure more than the sometimes-joys of barn cleaning and morning milking in February. These places make up the story of dairying as much as do the places where the joys of a June morning, the thrill of increased profits, the deep beauty of cows grazing, and the sense of feeding the world are felt. If we are to read Dairyland in all its complexity, we must learn to read the places where dairy stories ended as well as those where they still flourish.

William Seely's dairy story ended, but his daughter's dairy story continues. Mae Seely Sylvester is a daughter of Wisconsin dairying because she knows deeply what she learned on that farm, that "that which sustains us is something to which we must give care."

Did You Ever Milk a Cow?

The often-satisfying intimacy between human and cow at milking time

The successful dairyman must be a gentleman (gentle man). If he is rough and brutal with his cows he cannot secure the best results from them, as they will not do their best for the man who is unkind to them. In case a man cannot control his temper when milking, cannot resist the temptation to pound the cows with the milking stool, he should have a milking stool made so long and heavy that it cannot be used as a club.
—H. B. Gurler, *The Farm Dairy*, 1908

Milking a cow is the quintessential act of the dairy farmer, an intimate act where the human stands in for the cow's calf, inducing the cow to give human children what was intended for her own. The dairyman stimulates his cow to let down her milk through the same ancient emotional channels that would be used by her calf. To give milk, a cow must be calm, secure, and

continued . . .

touched. It is the dairy farmer's business to protect the cow's sense of motherhood.

However, stimulating maternity is not enough on a dairy farm, where infection, disease, and less-than-wholesome milk are just a microbe away. Preventing diseases of the udder, namely mastitis, can mean the difference between profit and loss for the farmer and between life and death (elimination from the herd) for the cow. Mastitis is a huge problem to be solved by management.

Many dairies milk three times a day. Cows give between 10 and 20 percent more milk with an extra milking. (But of course this requires more labor.) It is generally acknowledged that cows themselves benefit from more frequent milking.

Milking frequency is a management decision based on the farm's particular situation. For example, on farms practicing intensive grazing, cows spend their days too far from the milking parlor to make the trip three times a day. Some graziers are experimenting with less frequent milking, milking a cow, say, three times in two days. A few have gone back to milking only once a day.

Today, as in the past, the majority of dairy farmers do their own milking with the help of a hired hand or relative. Many farmers still milk in the "traditional" stall barn. Nearly all farmers have pipeline systems that carry the milk from the milking machine into a sealed refrigerated bulk tank. Often milk is metered at each

Photo by Mark Fay

Laura and John Stokke of Menomonie have milked together every day of their married lives. Twice a day. To say that their movements are practiced is to vastly understate the case. As this picture shows, the Stokkes enjoy the quintessential act of the dairy farmer.

Photo by Mark Fay

"Foster mothers of the human race" in John and Laura Stokke's barn

stanchion so the farmer can keep track of each cow's production.

But milking in a stanchion barn has been on the way out for some time. Today, more and more cows are milked in a parlor, where the milker stands at udder level to the cow. This has saved countless knees and has kept many farmers in dairying. Almost gone are the days when you could tell who had cows by his or her bent frame and slow gait.

Milking as an occupation for the dairy farmer is on its way out as well. A greater and greater percentage of our state's cows are milked by hired milkers, many of them Hispanic. As dairy farmers are relieved of their milking chores, they are freed to use their minds to better manage their herds, soil, and money. Many farmers miss the intimacy they had with their cows. None miss the pain.

Nature as practiced in Crawford County

Making It Pay, Again

꒰

Bob Molini

*[My son] and I were going to town to Wauzeka, and
we saw a guy on a Harley making a telephone call here in
the valley. And [since I've owned many Harleys] I stopped and
talked to him a little bit. And the conversation got to "What do you
do?" I said, "Well, I milk cows." He says, "Well, I feel sorry for you."
I said, "What?" I said, "Don't feel sorry for me, I'm having a great
time, I'm making money, and I hope I can do this until I'm ninety
years old." And the guy was stunned.* —Bob Molini

UNLIKE THE PRAIRIES and the smooth tabletop expanses of much
of Wisconsin's farmland, the unglaciated southwest quarter of the
state is land that nature has chosen not to improve very much for the
benefit of farmers and their modern machinery. It is land where the
firm voice of geology has said, "I'm allowing you only so much, and
no more." This is farmland most fitting for modest farmers like the
Amish. It is also a landscape most convivial to those in need of deep
breaths and the soul satisfactions of hidden valleys, winding roads,
and misty mornings.

That this land is unimproved for modern farming is not to suggest
that it hasn't supported dairying in the past, for it has. Immigrants
arrived, cows came, and the land yielded something of a living during
the time when "something of a living" was enough. But this is also a
place where many farming stories ended. In this modern era of intensity, this place steadfastly defies intensity. It just won't do here.

But the gospel of Wisconsin dairying is again being preached here—the same song played to a much older tune. The Good News of Dairying, to remind you, is the news that cows keep the soil and the farmer on the land. Late-nineteenth-century immigrants to our state were the first to hear this news telling them they could own land and make something of it if they kept cows. Today, a new wave of immigrants to Crawford County are hearing the Good News of Dairying. They are reclaiming land that might easily slip into a cow-less state. And they are making dairy farming pay—financially, socially, and spiritually.

Just four miles and sixty years from the now-reclaimed-by-nature Seely farm (see page 167) is the newly reclaimed farm of Bob Molini, his wife, Page, and his four sons, immigrants from modern life and the madding crowd. While William Seely's dairy story ended just down the road, Bob Molini's dairy story has begun. And so the greater dairy story continues.

In the early 1950s, when Bob was four, his father moved his family to an eighty-acre farm in Kenosha County, just over the Illinois line. Molini senior commuted to a job in a butcher shop in Chicago every day. The farm was his refuge and a place where he could accomplish something for himself. "It was," Bob says, "unbelievably beautiful country."

> When we moved out there we used to be able to count the number of cars that went by on our road. There was one or two a day. Unbelievable! And this is an area now where I go back there and I can hardly find my way around anymore. It's so developed. It is so busy, so much consumerism. It's really hard to believe that we can be producing and selling that much product—crap product, really. All that stuff we don't need, but it's there.

Bob's father kept a small herd of beef cattle, and before and after school Bob and his brothers performed many of the essential chores that kept the herd. On Sundays they had the great pleasure of working together with their father. They loved the land, and

Bribing Farmers to Save the Land: The Coon Valley
Watershed Soil Conservation Demonstration Project of 1933

By 1930 it had become clear to all except the ecologically blind

that southwestern Wisconsin's topsoil was slipping seaward.

—Aldo Leopold, *A Sand County Almanac*, 1949

Ernest Haugen was a boy of about eleven on his father's Coon Valley farm in 1933 when agents of the federal government and the University of Wisconsin, along with platoons of city boys, came to save Wisconsin farmers from themselves. After years of being not-so-thoughtfully farmed, the rolling hills of the Coulee Region of southwest Wisconsin were washing away. Poor farming practices such as planting row crops up and down hills rather than contoured to them, losing the ground cover on hillsides by overgrazing cattle in woodlands, and failing to replenish the soil with clover or alfalfa had put this graceful land onto the endangered list. So, deep into the Great Depression with its visions of soil blowing away in great dust bowls, the U.S. Department of Agriculture created the U.S. Soil Erosion Service. Coon Valley was chosen as its first demonstration project.

As Haugen remembers in this oral history interview from February 2010, it was the "greatest thing that ever happened."

Haugen: We had a very dry year in 1934. [He probably means 1933.] Very hot and dry. So the hay was very short. We had twenty-one loads of hay. Year after [we] joined the Soil Conservation, [we and our neighbors] raised a lot of alfalfa hay. Had a lot of loads of hay. From 1934 to 1935, [we] had over a hundred loads of loose hay.

[My father] learned a lot from soil conservation. The terracing was very good, and they fenced off the woodlots to prevent the cows from going in there. Because when the cows went in there, the grass got all eaten and the soil ran down. And when [cows] pasture in the timber, they get all scratched up. They get sore teats. Difficult to milk.

So was your father happy to have all this work done for him and to fix up his land?

Yes, by the Soil Conservation. Greatest thing that ever happened. . . . We got three hundred pounds of lime free, and all the

continued . . .

grass seed was free, and the fence that was put up by the CCC [Civilian Conservation Corps] was free. All the work was done free. The putting up [of] the fence was free. Oh yeah . . . that was worth a lot.

Was the land improved? Did you get better yields?

Yes, much better. Yeah, the neighbors, the ones who did not join up, they saw [that] the ones who joined the Soil Conservation had bigger yields to produce more hay and [that] they practiced rotational crops.

Were some farmers in that day still not doing rotational crops?

Some had the habit of growing corn year after year. Maybe several years. And that produces more soil erosion.

Were some of your neighbors opposed to this? They didn't like this government plan, right?

Oh yes. . . . Well, there were rumors that the government would take the land away. That those government men would come back and, if they were not good farmers, would take the land away. [My father] used to be against everything, but it was a very great thing he did.

The great lesson of dairying is that deposits in the bank of the future improve yields—and improved yields improve lives. Farmers, like all human beings, often need to be bribed and regulated to protect the future. This, too, is part of the progressives' project, as was the Coon Valley Watershed Soil Conservation Demonstration Project. It was "a very great thing."

they loved working on it. For Bob, it is a land and a life remembered—deeply.

During the 1960s, while getting his degree at the University of Wisconsin in La Crosse, Bob fell in love with nature as practiced in the Coulee Region of our state. This having been the Age of Aquarius and all, Bob also fell under the sway of the new and powerful idea that life can be fun. After college he moved back to the farm in Kenosha, where he set about enjoying himself by hunting and hugging trees, a practice he continues today:

Many times I shut off the tractor out there and just climb up on a tree—actually, I still climb trees. I'm sixty years old. I will still climb a tree and hug a tree and just feel the movement. That's when I feel the fullest and the most alive, of course. And the silence—that's what

it's all about: listening to nature sounds, and a little bit of silence. It's like a meditation, really. It's inspirational. You're actually being inspired by it.

A farm reclaimed for cows: Bob and Page Molini's place, where a story continues

Back in Kenosha, Bob was making his job as a high school science teacher fun, too, until, that is, his fun began to run him aground against the Piscean-age school administration who, apparently, did not get the meaning of the T-shirt Bob wore one day proclaiming "Everything is Energy." Nor did his principal appreciate Bob telling the daughter of a powerful PTO member that plagiarizing a term paper was not good for her character.

She brought me the paper, and I just crumpled it up and threw it into the garbage can. I said, "That's garbage. That's where it's going to go 'cause you copied that. You're an intelligent girl; now do it right this time." And between classes she called her mother. I never got any support from my principal. It was unbelievable.

For those too young to remember or too old to want to, I'll remind you that many people during this time were hearing the call to "heal" the schism between the spiritual and the physical world. For those committed to this healing, understanding that "everything is energy" meant looking for ways to live a soul-satisfying life. The herd of consumers and the putting-your-child's-résumé-over-her-character types sent sensitive souls elsewhere for their sustenance. People who understood the equality of life and energy were also beginning to realize that they were what they ate. For these people, food became a spiritual path, the better to bring body and soul together.

How his food was grown and what he thought about it began to really matter to Bob Molini. So in 1994 he transferred his hopes for natural living to the beautiful hills outside Wauzeka, where he could put his own food where his mouth was. He moved his family to a place where they could live and work harmoniously with the more convivial energies of life.

They chose a fallen farm, one in danger of being reclaimed by trees, where Bob could, as the farmers say, "keep the farm milking" by making only modest demands on it. This was a farm Bob could reclaim by returning it to the level of productivity it had originally supported, and no more. And it was a farm he could make pay, because it would support his modest material needs while paying huge personal dividends.

Photo by Mark Fay

This was a farm Bob could make spiritual and on which he could have fun—and provide a more natural life for his sons.

And, this was a place where the old gospel of a-good-life-through-cows could be quietly preached to young farmers looking to stay on the land and to émigrés escaping modernity. Bob, still a teacher, preaches and teaches the new gospel of laid-back dairying and the redemption of old land through old methods.

Bob Molini practices "postmodern" dairying in that he consciously turns his back on the kind of farming that makes strong demands on land, on animals, and especially on farmers, whom he believes can and should live harmoniously with nature—the better to produce food worth eating and to live a life worth living.

To go forward to new premodern times, Bob has eschewed nearly each of the points in the improved dairying program that has defined "progressive dairying" since W. D. Hoard and the founders

Bob and Page Molini put their own food where their mouths are. They raise hogs and beef cattle for their table as well as chickens and ducks and biodynamic vegetables. Theirs is a diversified farm of the old school with all of the satisfactions that come from self-sufficiency. I think that's why Page is smiling.

A Lecture-Discussion Program Sponsored by
Crawford Stewardship Project and Valley Stewardship Network

The Good News About
Farming
Fun and Abundance
Monday Evening May 5, 2008
6:30-9:00
Seneca Town Hall
(off Taylor Ridge Road across from Seneca H.S. ballfield)
featured speakers
Bob Molini & Page Brady, Remnant Ridge Organic
Family Farm
Eric & Lisa Klein, Hidden Stream Farm
Lori & Alan Callister
Kevin & Mary Yanke, A Grazing Place Farm
John & Virginia Goeke, Sylvan Meadows Farm

Tuesday May 6, 2008 Pasture Walk at the Molini Farm
10:00 AM – 2:00 PM

Bob Molini teaches
fun and abundance in
Crawford County.

turned Wisconsin farmers away from the economic and environmental train wreck they were headed for in the 1870s. Bob decided to lighten the intense relationship that has made cow and human business partners in an efficient, modern enterprise. To wit:

In 2007 the average dairy cow on a Wisconsin farm produced just more than nineteen thousand pounds of milk a year. The average herd was eighty-eight. Bob Molini has twenty-four milking cows each giving seven thousand pounds of milk. (In the early 1950s, Wisconsin cows began to exceed seven thousand pounds a year. They have not looked back.)[1]

The great transition to modern full-time dairy farming began when farmers found ways to keep cows in milk year-round as they passed beyond the ancient seasonal nature of exclusively grass-based herding. Keeping cows in milk during Wisconsin winters meant cultivating forage and grain crops whose food value would exceed a cow's nutrition needs.

Just as William Seely had no silo, neither does Bob Molini. And he grows no corn for his cows—only for his hogs, chickens, and geese. Bob's cows graze. During the winter they are kept in health—but not in milk—by his hay crop.

Year-round milking means year-round calving and year-round freshening. Bob dries his cows up for the winter. They calve only in the spring. "I love it," he says.

All the calves are born during those four to six weeks from March through April. That's my time. There are many advantages to it. Gives me time off in the wintertime to be able to do things, to be able to recharge and get ready for spring. To me, I'm as excited about

starting milking as I am about ending milking. You know. To me it's a no-brainer. So refreshing. If I thought I had to milk cows twice a day, every day for the rest of my life, I don't think I could do it.

It's a time too for intellectual growth and spiritual growth. If we're working all the time, you don't have the time. You don't have the time to grow.

Bob and his cows take their vacations together. He sells no milk during the winter.

To feed cows year-round, to protect them from extreme temperatures, to minister to their needs, and to keep them handy for milking, farmers built dairy barns. Other than the very worst days of winter, Bob's cows are outside except when they come in to be milked by milking machines in the parlor. And Bob milks just once

A premodern dairyman—the ideal model for postmodern dairymen like Bob Molini a day, usually in the evening, unless he wants to see one of his sons' teams play.

Calves on most Wisconsin dairy farms are separated from their mothers almost immediately after she licks them off. This is one of the seemingly brutal but necessary acts a farmer does for his own benefit. Bob, on the other hand, keeps his calves on their mother for as long as they want. He figures he loses one thousand pounds of milk per cow but gains healthier young stock. Indeed, he believes leaving mother and calf together keeps the fabric of nature from rending. Keeping nature whole is very important to Bob and like-minded dairy farmers.

After improved feeding, the genetic improvement of dairy stock was the second pillar of the modern dairy industry. Today nearly all breeding is done artificially. Improving the herd through conscious breeding is one of the full-time occupations on a dairy farm, whether it is done by the farmer or by hired professional experts. It takes great attention, day in and day out. Bob runs two or three bulls: "It's such a time-saver." Bob is buying time for himself and his sons.

And he is making a living from it. His costs are very low compared to conventionally intense dairy operations situated on valuable dairy land. By milking only once a day he saves on electricity to run his milk cooling tank and his milking machines and on the costs for chemicals to keep his milking equipment sanitary. He pays not a cent for "genetic services," and he spends nothing for the vet because he feels his herd is healthy "naturally." And because he grows no corn, he fuels no tractor to produce it. (He does use a tractor to cut and bale hay.)

And Bob sells his milk into the commercial organic market, which pays him a premium price.

Organic Valley, one of the country's most successful organic milk co-ops, is nearby in Vernon County. Organic Valley has done much to keep modest farms in southwest Wisconsin like Bob Molini's in milk. Not only does the company pay sometimes significantly higher prices for milk, it also sponsors educational efforts to help farmers make the most of their land and cows, organically speaking. The premium price paid for organic milk and the more laid-back approach organic farming demands allow farmers like Bob Molini the freedom to farm in a way that matches their personalities.

> I've bought myself freedom and quality of life. Time for spiritual development. Loving life, you know! And it's all fallen into place. I've done it. But my big thing [is], I just want to spread the word.

Bob has accomplished two very good things in his decade as a dairy farmer: First, he has redeemed a fallen farm by asking no more from it than it can bear, reclaiming a place for the honest work cows provide. He has kept it milking. And second, he has found a way for certain modest souls to enjoy an income by being among cows and grass. Bob teaches the good news about farming to interested local young people looking for a way to stay in dairying without going broke and being broken by the labor. He says,

> The concept that you have to work seventeen or twenty hours a day, 365 days a year for the rest of your life, that doesn't have to be. There's many other different ways of doing it. And I keep talking about quality of life. I'm doing it, and I've got quality of life, and I've got it for my boys. And farming can be that way. But I'm trying to tell these younger farmers that to me it's a no-brainer. Maybe you start milking cows once a day. Okay? They're young, they've got a lot of energy. They can be working an eight-hour day somewhere else and milk at five o'clock, six o'clock at night. So you're making two incomes, and you're slowly buying your dad off for five years you're working at this. And finally you've got enough money to get started—and continue that once-a-day milking.

Bob helps former city people prepare for small-scale dairying by conducting "pasture walks" on his farm. He teaches about good

Trying to Get More for Farmers: Organic Valley Cooperative

In the late 1960s, the state and federal government made plans to dam a huge area of the flood-prone Kickapoo Valley in the beautiful unglaciated area of southwest Wisconsin. The project would create a large recreational lake and eliminate flood insurance claims and expensive reconstruction projects. During this same period, the Kickapoo Valley had become something of a magnet for spiritually minded, educated city people escaping the crowds for simpler, less industrial lives. These settlers and many other residents of the area were against the government's plan.

Opponents of the project succeeded, leaving the marginal dairy land of the valley to the Amish with their nonmechanized practices, small-scale beef raisers, traditional and hippie dairy farmers, and hobby farmers. These groups, which didn't always play well with one another at the time, were united in their desire to see the land stay rustic and bucolic. To preserve the land, they needed to find ways to make marginal dairy land, small herds, and a less mechanized pace pay much better. Kickapoo Valley dairy farmers were simply not competitive with increasingly efficient international agriculture.

The farmers needed to transcend commodity milk prices by adding new value to milk. In addition, many of these farmers and rural enthusiasts believed the world itself would be a better place if dairy farming could be done using less-intensive approaches to cultivation, herding, and community.

Organic Valley Cooperative was founded in LaFarge in 1988 to make Coulee Region farmers more profitable and to make the world a better place for farming. The co-op and others in the organic movement were looking for enough consumers who believed they and the world would benefit if they paid higher prices for milk that was certified "more beneficial."

Today, Organic Valley Cooperative has more than 1,600 members in thirty-three states and four Canadian provinces.[1] Sales reached $528 million in 2008.[2] Obviously, the idea that consumers would pay more to support a certain vision of agriculture has proved true. In supporting this idea, both the consumers and the co-op believe they are making the world a better place.

1. Organic Valley Cooperative, "About Organic Valley," www.organicvalley.coop/newsroom/about-organic -valley/.
2. Organic Valley Cooperative, "Organic Valley Farmer -Owners Celebrate $528 Million in 2008 Sales While Keeping 58 Million Pounds of Synthetic Chemicals Off the Land," press release, April 2, 2009, www .organicvalley.coop/newsroom/press-releases/details/ article/organic-valley-farmer-owners-celebrate-528 -million-in-2008-sales-while-keeping-58-million -pounds-of/.

pastures and unobtrusive husbandry. He teaches how to care for cows without disturbing very much at all. He says,

> I don't like to get on my soapbox, but this time I will. I do like to share this word. And share this joy that I'm having with this experience.

Bob Molini shares the good news that dairying can be a life of fun and abundance—the gospel of dairying sung to an older tune.

Champion milker, 1931

Notes

꙳

The Wisconsin Idea of Dairying: A Brief History

1. Harva Hachten and Terese Allen, *The Flavor of Wisconsin: An Informal History of Food and Eating in the Badger State*, rev. and exp. ed. (Madison: Wisconsin Historical Society Press, 2009), 64.

2. Joseph Schafer, *A History of Agriculture in Wisconsin*, Wisconsin Domesday Book, General Studies 1 (Madison: State Historical Society of Wisconsin, 1922), 92.

3. Eric E. Lampard, *The Rise of the Dairy Industry in Wisconsin: A Study in Agricultural Change, 1820–1920* (Madison: State Historical Society of Wisconsin, 1963), 23.

4. Wisconsin State Agricultural Society, "A Review of This Period," in *Transactions of the Wisconsin State Agricultural Society . . .* (Madison: Atwood and Rublee, 1857), 106.

5. W. A. Titus, "The Westward Trail," *Wisconsin Magazine of History* 20, no. 3 (March 1937): 310–22.

6. Schafer, *History of Agriculture*, 97.

7. Ibid.

8. Richard N. Current, *The Civil War Era, 1848–1873*, vol. 2, *The History of Wisconsin*, ed. William Fletcher Thompson (Madison: State Historical Society of Wisconsin, 1976), 378.

9. Lampard, *Rise of the Dairy Industry*, 71.

10. W. D. Hoard, *Hoard's Dairyman*, January 4, 1889.

11. Robert C. Nesbit, *Wisconsin: A History*, 2nd ed. (Madison: University of Wisconsin Press, 1989), 284.

12. Thomas Pederson, "Some Recollections of Thomas Pederson," pt. 1, *Wisconsin Magazine of History* 21, no. 1 (September 1937): 33.

13. Ibid., pt. 3, *Wisconsin Magazine of History* 21, no. 3 (March 1938): 308.

14. J. Q. Emery, "President's Address," in *Thirty-second Annual Report of the Wisconsin Dairymen's Association . . .*, comp. George W. Burchard (Madison: Democrat Printing, 1904), 26–27.

15. W. A. Henry, "Dairy Experiments," in *Twelfth Annual Report of the Wisconsin Dairymen's Association . . .* , comp. D. W. Curtis (Madison: Democrat Printing, 1884), 105.

16. W. A. Henry, "The Importance of Co-operation Among Dairy Farmers," in *Thirty-fourth Annual Report of the Wisconsin Dairymen's Association . . .* , comp. George W. Burchard (Madison: Democrat Printing, 1906), 170.

17. X. A. Willard, *Willard's Practical Dairy Husbandry* (New York: D. D. T. Moore, 1872), 10.

18. Lampard, *Rise of the Dairy Industry*, 123, 142.

19. Ibid., 232.

20. U.S. Bureau of the Census, *Twelfth Census of the United States, Taken in the Year 1900, vol. 5, Agriculture, Part 1: Farms, Livestock, and Animal Products* (Washington, DC: Government Printing Office, 1902), 914.

21. Carl E. Coppock, "Selected Features of the U.S. Dairy Industry from 1900 to 2000" (address, annual Southwest Nutrition and Management Conference, Phoenix, AZ, February 24–25, 2000), Table 1.

22. John A. Cross, "Change in America's Dairyland," *Geographical Review* 91, no. 4 (October 2001): 703, table 1.

23. USDA/National Agricultural Statistics Service, "Milk, All, Prices Received by Farmers, Wisconsin," www.nass.usda.gov/Statistics_by _State/Wisconsin/Publications/Dairy/mkallpri.pdf.

24. Cross, "Change in America's Dairyland."

25. Paul O. Nyhus, "Wisconsin Agricultural Statistics," in *Wisconsin Blue Book*, ed. Fred L. Holmes (Madison: State Printing Board, 1925), 326.

26. Lampard, *Rise of the Dairy Industry*, 449, table B-1.

27. Ibid., 453, table E.

28. Ibid.

29. Ibid.

30. Loyal Durand Jr., "The Cheese Manufacturing Regions of Wisconsin, 1850–1950," in *Transactions of the Wisconsin Academy of Sciences, Arts and Letters*, vol. 42 (Madison: Wisconsin Academy of Sciences, Arts and Letters, 1953), 129.

31. J. Q. Emery, "The Wonderful Story of Wisconsin's Dairy Industry," in *Wisconsin Blue Book*, ed. Fred L. Holmes (Madison: State Printing Board, 1925), 305–6.

32. Ibid., 298.

33. Bob Cropp and Truman Graf, "The History and Role of Dairy Co-operatives," University of Wisconsin Center for Cooperatives, www.uwcc.wisc.edu/info/dairy/history.pdf, 7, table 1.

34. Paul R. Voss, Daniel L. Veroff, and David D. Long, "Wisconsin's People: A Portrait of Wisconsin's Population on the Threshold of the 21st Century," in *Wisconsin Blue Book* (Madison: Wisconsin Legislative Reference Bureau, 2003–2004), 108–13.

35. Cross, "Change in America's Dairyland."

36. Ibid.

37. USDA/National Agricultural Statistics Service, "Quick Stats," www.nass.usda.gov/Data_and_Statistics/Quick_Stats/index.asp.

38. U.S. Bureau of Labor Statistics, *Bulletin of the United States Bureau of Labor Statistics*, no. 315 (January 1923): 57, table 7.

Finding Themselves on the Farm: Saxon Homestead Farm

1. Mrs. D. Huntley, "Farmers' Boys and Girls," in *Fifth Annual Report of the Wisconsin Dairymen's Association . . .* , comp. D. W. Curtis (Madison: David Atwood, 1877), 47.

The Business of Progressives: The Crave Brothers

1. Focus on Energy, "Crave Brothers Farm Reaps Big Benefits with Energy Efficiency and Renewable Energy" (Wisconsin Focus on Energy, 2009), www.focusonenergy.com/files/Document_Management_System/Renewables/cravebrothersfarm_casestudy.pdf.

The Ages of Cheddar: Sam Cook and Sid Cook

1. Eric E. Lampard, *The Rise of the Dairy Industry in Wisconsin: A Study in Agricultural Change, 1820–1920* (Madison: State Historical Society of Wisconsin, 1963), 453, table E.

Making It Pay, Again: Bob Molini

1. USDA/National Agricultural Statistics Service, "Milk Production per Cow, Wisconsin," www.nass.usda.gov/Statistics_by_State/Wisconsin/Publications/Dairy/mkpercow.pdf.

Cooling room at Coldren Cheese Company of Brodhead, Wisconsin, date unknown

Bibliography

Allerton, E. P. "Dairy Factory System—a Blessing to the Farmer's Wife." In Wisconsin Dairymen's Association, *Third Annual Report of the Wisconsin Dairymen's Association* . . . , 17–20. Fort Atkinson, WI: W. D. Hoard, 1875.

Bailey, John M. *The Book of Ensilage; or, The New Dispensation for Farmers*. New York: Orange Judd, 1881.

Bennett, A. I. "Industry of Rock County." In *Transactions of the Wisconsin State Agricultural Society, with an Abstract of the Returns of County Societies and Kindred Associations, Together with Reports of the Industry of Counties*. Vol. 6, 1860, edited by J. W. Hoyt, 320–24. Madison: Smith and Cullaton, 1861.

Burchard, George W., comp. *Thirty-fourth Annual Report of the Wisconsin Dairymen's Association Held at Waukesha, Wis., January 31, February 1 and 2, 1905. Report of the Proceedings, Annual Address of the President, and Interesting Essays and Discussions Relating to the Dairy Interests*. Madison: Democrat Printing, 1906.

Clapp, I. J. "The Influence of the Dairy Business upon the Farm and Farmer." In D. W. Curtis, *Seventh Annual Report of the Wisconsin Dairymen's Association* . . . , 22–28. Madison: David Atwood, 1879.

Coppock, Carl E. "Selected Features of the U.S. Dairy Industry from 1900 to 2000." Address, annual Southwest Nutrition and Management Conference, Phoenix, AZ, February 24–25, 2000.

"Crop and Livestock Man-hours Down." *Wisconsin Crop and Livestock Reporter*, July 1963, 30.

Cropp, Bob, and Truman Graf. "The History and Role of Dairy Cooperatives." University of Wisconsin Center for Cooperatives. www.uwcc.wisc.edu/info/dairy/history.pdf.

Cross, John A. "Change in America's Dairyland." *Geographical Review* 91, no. 4 (October 2001): 702–14.

Current, Richard N. *The Civil War Era, 1848-1873.* Vol. 2, *The History of Wisconsin*, edited by William Fletcher Thompson. Madison: State Historical Society of Wisconsin, 1976.

Curtis, D. W., comp. *Seventh Annual Report of the Wisconsin Dairymen's Association, Held at Kenosha, Wis., January 22–23, 1879. Report of Proceedings, Annual Address of the President, and Interesting Essays Relating to the Dairy Interests.* Madison: David Atwood, 1879.

"The Difference in Farmers and Farm Management." *Hoard's Dairyman*, November 29, 1912.

Drake, H. C. "The Essential Elements of a Good Dairyman." In Wisconsin Dairymen's Association, *Third Annual Report of the Wisconsin Dairymen's Association . . .* , 25–28. Fort Atkinson, WI: W. D. Hoard, 1875.

Durand, Loyal, Jr. "The Cheese Manufacturing Regions of Wisconsin, 1850–1950." In *Transactions of the Wisconsin Academy of Sciences, Arts and Letters.* Vol. 42, 109–30. Madison: Wisconsin Academy of Sciences, Arts and Letters, 1953.

Emery, J. Q. "The Growth and the Present Status of the Dairy Industry in Wisconsin." In *Thirty-eighth Annual Report of the Wisconsin Dairymen's Association Held at West Salem, Wis., February 9, 10 and 11, 1910. Report of the Proceedings, Annual Address of the President, Interesting Essays and Discussions Relating to the Dairy Interests*, compiled by A. J. Glover, 127–37. Madison: Democrat Printing, 1910.

———. "President's Address." In *Thirty-second Annual Report of the Wisconsin Dairymen's Association Held at Platteville, Wis., February 10, 11 and 12, 1904. Report of the Proceedings, Annual Address of the President, and Interesting Essays and Discussions Relating to the Dairy Interests*, compiled by George W. Burchard, 17–27. Madison: Democrat Printing, 1904.

Emery, Mrs. J. Q. "The Living Proposition of a Dairy Farm." In George W. Burchard, *Thirty-fourth Annual Report of the Wisconsin Dairymen's Association . . .* , 51–65. Madison, Democrat Printing, 1906.

———. "The Wonderful Story of Wisconsin's Dairy Industry." In *Wisconsin Blue Book*, edited by Fred L. Holmes, 297–307. Madison: State Printing Board, 1925.

Focus on Energy. "Crave Brothers Farm Reaps Big Benefits with Energy Efficiency and Renewable Energy." Wisconsin Focus on Energy, 2009. www.focusonenergy.com/files/Document_Management_System/ Renewables/cravebrothersfarm_casestudy.pdf.

Gurler, H. B. *The Farm Dairy*. Chicago: Breeder's Gazette, 1908.

Hachten, Harva, and Terese Allen. *The Flavor of Wisconsin: An Informal History of Food and Eating in the Badger State*. Rev. and exp. ed. Madison: Wisconsin Historical Society Press, 2009.

Haugen, Ernest. Interview with author. 2009.

Henry, W. A. "Dairy Experiments." In *Twelfth Annual Report of the Wisconsin Dairymen's Association, Held at Lake Mills, Wis., January 16, 17 and 18, 1884. Report of the Proceedings, Annual Address of the President, and Interesting Essays Relating to the Dairy Interests*, compiled by D. W. Curtis, 103–5. Madison: Democrat Printing, 1884.

———. "The Importance of Co-operation Among Dairy Farmers." In George W. Burchard, *Thirty-fourth Annual Report of the Wisconsin Dairymen's Association . . .* , 168–76. Madison: Democrat Printing, 1906.

Hoard, W. D. "The History of the Dairy Interest in Wisconsin." In D. W. Curtis, *Seventh Annual Report of the Wisconsin Dairymen's Association . . .* , 128–29. Madison: David Atwood, 1879.

Hoard, W. D. *Jefferson County Union*, January 4, 1889.

Hofstadter, Richard. *The Age of Reform: From Bryan to F. D. R.* New York: Knopf, 1956.

Huntley, Mrs. D. "Farmers' Boys and Girls." In *Fifth Annual Report of the Wisconsin Dairymen's Association, Held at Appleton, Wis., January 17 and 18, 1877. Report of Proceedings, Annual Address of the President, and Interesting Essays, Relating to the Dairy Interests*, compiled by D. W. Curtis, 46–54. Madison: David Atwood, 1877.

"Kraft Recalls Rise of Cheese Industry." *New York Times*, February 26, 1928.

Lampard, Eric E. *The Rise of the Dairy Industry in Wisconsin: A Study in Agricultural Change, 1820–1920*. Madison: State Historical Society of Wisconsin, 1963.

Lane, Clarence B. *The Business of Dairying: How to Conduct Dairy Farming for the Largest Profit*. New York: Orange Judd, 1909.

Leopold, Aldo. *A Sand County Almanac and Sketches Here and There*. London: Oxford University Press, 1949.

McCarthy, Charles. *The Wisconsin Idea*. New York: Macmillian, 1912.

Morse, John T., Jr. *Life and Letters of Oliver Wendell Holmes*. Vol 1. Cambridge, MA: Riverside, 1896.

Nesbit, Robert C. *Wisconsin: A History*. 2nd ed. Madison: University of Wisconsin Press, 1989.

New York State Dairymen's Association, *Fifteenth Annual Report of the New York State Dairymen's Association. With Transactions and Addresses, for the Year 1891.* Utica, NY: Utica Herald, 1892.

Nyhus, Paul O. "Wisconsin Agricultural Statistics." In *Wisconsin Blue Book,* edited by Fred L. Holmes, 323–30. Madison: State Printing Board, 1925.

———. "Wisconsin Agricultural Statistics." In *Wisconsin Blue Book,* edited by Fred L. Holmes, 285–95. Madison: State Printing Board, 1927.

Oncken, John. Interview with author. March 2010.

Organic Valley Cooperative. "About Organic Valley." www.organicvalley .coop/newsroom/about-organic-valley/.

———. "Organic Valley Farmer-Owners Celebrate $528 Million in 2008 Sales While Keeping 58 Million Pounds of Synthetic Chemicals Off the Land." Press release, April 2, 2009. www.organicvalley.coop/ newsroom/press-releases/details/article/organic-valley-farmer -owners-celebrate-528-million-in-2008-sales-while-keeping -58-million-pounds-of/.

Pederson, Thomas. "Some Reflections of Thomas Pederson." Pts. 1 and 3. *Wisconsin Magazine of History* 21, no. 1 (September 1937): 16–34; 21, no. 3 (March 1938): 301–21.

Philips, A. J. *Queen Vashti: The Autobiography of a Guernsey Cow.* West Salem, WI: A. J. Philips [1906?].

Roberts, Isaac Phillips. *The Farmstead: The Making of the Rural Home and the Lay-out of the Farm.* New York: Macmillan, 1900.

Schafer, Joseph. *A History of Agriculture in Wisconsin.* Wisconsin Domesday Book, General Studies 1. Madison: State Historical Society of Wisconsin, 1922.

Smith, Hiram. "Experience with Fodder Corn and the Silo." In *Wisconsin Farmers' Institutes, 1888. Bulletin No. 2,* edited by W. H. Morrison, 49–54. Madison: Western Farmer, 1888.

Titus, W. A. "The Westward Trail." *Wisconsin Magazine of History* 20, no. 3 (March 1937): 310–22.

U.S. Bureau of the Census. *Twelfth Census of the United States, Taken in the Year 1900. Vol. 5, Agriculture, Part 1: Farms, Livestock, and Animal Products.* Washington, DC: Government Printing Office, 1902.

U.S. Bureau of Labor Statistics. *Bulletin of the United States Bureau of Labor Statistics,* no. 315 (January 1923).

USDA/National Agricultural Statistics Service. "2007 Dairy Producer
   Survey." July 2007. www.nass.usda.gov/Statistics_by_State/Wisconsin/
   Publications/Dairy/dairyproducer2007.pdf.

———. "Milk, All, Prices Received by Farmers, Wisconsin." www.nass.usda
   .gov/Statistics_by_State/Wisconsin/Publications/Dairy/mkallpri.pdf.

———. "Milk Production per Cow, Wisconsin." www.nass.usda.gov/
   Statistics_by_State/Wisconsin/Publications/Dairy/mkpercow.pdf.

———. "Quick Stats." www.nass.usda.gov/Data_and_Statistics/Quick
   _Stats/index.asp.

Van Wagenen, Jared. *The Cow*. New York: Macmillan, 1922.

Voss, Paul R., Daniel L. Veroff, and David D. Long. "Wisconsin's People:
   A Portrait of Wisconsin's Population on the Threshold of the 21st
   Century." In *Wisconsin Blue Book*, 99–174. Madison: Wisconsin
   Legislative Reference Bureau, 2003–2004.

Washburn, R. M. *Productive Dairying*. Philadelphia: J. B. Lippincott, 1917.

White, W. C. "Butter and Cheese Making." In D. W. Curtis, *Seventh Annual
   Report of the Wisconsin Dairymen's Association . . .* , 28–31. Madison:
   David Atwood, 1879.

Willard, X. A. *Willard's Practical Dairy Husbandry: A Complete Treatise
   on Dairy Farms and Farming,—Dairy Stock and Stock Feeding,—Milk,
   Its Management and Manufacture into Butter and Cheese,—History
   and Mode of Organization of Cheese Factories,—Dairy Utenciles, Etc.,
   Etc.* 3rd ed. New York: D. D. T. Moore, 1872.

Wisconsin Dairymen's Association. *Third Annual Report of the Wisconsin
   Dairymen's Association, with a Record of the Annual Meeting Held at
   Fort Atkinson, Wisconsin, February 3rd and 4th and 17th and 18th,
   1875.* Fort Atkinson, WI: W. D. Hoard, 1875.

Wisconsin State Agricultural Society. "A Review of This Period." In
   *Transactions of the Wisconsin State Agricultural Society. For the
   Years 1854-5-6-7.* 101–6. Madison: Atwood and Rublee, 1857.

Index

organic movement, 87–88,
    188–189, 190
Organic Valley Cooperative,
    188–189, 190

pasteurization, 38, 48, 101
Patenaude, Dan, *126*, 127–139
Patenaude, Jeanne, 128
patience, 119–122
Pederson, Thomas, 23
Philips, A. J., xiii, 174
Pickett family, 12
Pleasant Ridge Reserve, 137–139
power sources, *55–56*
production: control of, 47–52;
    Crave brothers and, 84–85;
    feed and, 71–72; grazing and,
    75; of milk, 32, 53
Professional Dairy Producers of
    Wisconsin, 153
progressivism: Crave brothers
    and, 79–93; Dan Patenaude
    and Mike Gingrich and,
    127–129; intelligent design
    and, 145–146; Mayer family
    and, 151–153; overview of,
    18–20; Saxon Homestead
    Farm and, 64–65
Prussian enlightenment, 18–19

Ramirez, Marisol, *121*
Roberts, Isaac Phillips, 80,
    156, 172, 184
Rockwell, Charles, 12
rotational grazing, 132–133

Saxon Homestead Farm, 33,
    61–77, *62*, 135
Schafer, Joseph, 6
Searls, Jarred, 115–117
Searls, Julia, *115*
Seely, William, 167–174, *169*

selection, of dairy cows, 145–146
short course. *See* education,
    in farming; University of
    Wisconsin
showing cows, 110, *111*, 142, 144,
    144, 149–150, *149*, 157–158
silos, 26, 27–28, *28*, 29, 64, *66*, *136*
Sixel, Bill, *72*
Smith, Hiram, 12, 27, 36, 97
Smith-Lever Act (1914), 30
soil: conservation of, 46–47,
    181–182; renewing, 9–10, 23–24
specialization, 36–38, 56, 135
Stokke, John, *176*, *177*
Stokke, Laura, *176*, *177*
sustainability, 67–68
Sylvester, Mae Seely, 167,
    168–173, *173*

Titus, W. A., 8
tractors, 56
Truttmann, Dan, 132, *132*

university education, 30–35,
    113–114
University of Wisconsin, 30–31
U.S. Soil Erosion Service, 181–182

Van Wagenen, Jared, 1, 131

Washburn, R. M., 162
weed control, chemical, 54, 56, 68
Weeks, Dr., 27
wheat, 6–8, *7*, 23
White, W. C., 22
winter feeding, 25–28, 29,
    186–187
Wisconsin: as Dairyland, 44–46;
    decline of dairy farms in, 50;
    impact of dairy cows on, xiii–
    xiv, 2–5; sources of farming
    income in, *47*

About the Author

Photo by Joel Heiman

GROWING UP NEAR WASHINGTON, DC, Ed Janus knew the front end of a cow from the back—and that was it. But after getting his degree in anthropology and working as a community organizer and bus driver in Chicago, he became a dairy farmer in Crawford County, Wisconsin. There he fell in love with cows, fields, barns, and dairy farmers.

After two years of milking, plowing, hefting, scraping, and spreading, Ed left farming, but not his love of it. He started the Madison Muskies, a minor league baseball team, and Capital Brewery, now one of the country's top-ranked breweries. He has spent the last twenty years interviewing hundreds of people as an audio journalist, writer, and oral historian and has created radio programs for public radio, the Voice of America, and publishers in the United States and Germany. His first-person audio book on surviving breast cancer won top honors from the Audio Publishers Association in 1999.

In 2007 Ed created a series of audio profiles of today's dairy farmers and cheesemakers for the Wisconsin Milk Marketing Board. While preparing these stories, he realized that it is impossible to understand the present without examining the deeper soil of the past from which it has grown.

Today Ed is working to preserve that deeper soil through his oral history organization, the Wisconsin Dairy History Project. By recording the older voices of dairying before they disappear, he hopes to leave future historians a trove of authentic first-person accounts of the people who created Dairyland, so that we can understand the present by understanding our past.